Walter Jamieson, Editor

Community Destination Management in Developing Economies

Pre-publication
REVIEWS,
COMMENTARIES,
EVALUATIONS . . .

"This book will be useful for undergraduates in the fields of both tourism and development. Through a series of diverse chapters, the book flags a number of issues faced by tourism managers in the developing world.

Its value lies in the empirical case studies from developing economies such as Thailand and Cambodia. These illustrate the obstacles and opportunities for tourism to contribute to sustainable development in such destinations. Of particular interest are the discussions about how tourism may be linked with traditional economic and cultural activities in developing economies: for example, how synergies may be developed between tourism and agriculture. There are also important chapters that address the less glamorous but practical aspects of tourism development such as solid waste management, energy and transport management, and the mitigation of harmful socioeconomic impacts.

While the book focuses on developing economies in South East Asia, there are also chapters that have application for students and practitioners of destination management in general. These highlight a range of useful tools that may be employed to assist destination development: for example, there are useful discussions of the value of interpretation, about festivals and events, and on governance and the role of community participation. Two interesting chapters address the potential of GIS and computer visualization technology for destination management."

Brent Lovelock, PhD
Senior Lecturer, Department
of Tourism, University of Otago

More pre-publication
REVIEWS, COMMENTARIES, EVALUATIONS . . .

"**C**ommunity Destination Management in Developing Economies presents a comprehensive approach to destination management in urban and rural areas, including relevant cases and illustrations from Southeast Asia. The editor has assembled an excellent collection of materials relevant to meeting the challenges of managing tourism at the local level to achieve sustainable environmental, social, and economic goals. Of particular interest to readers may be the sections focused on facilitating a quality visitor experience; effective interpretation techniques; GIS and remote sensing tools; and the use of visualization and scenarios in tourism planning."

Donald E. Hawkins, EdD
Eisenhower Professor of Tourism Policy,
School of Business, George
Washington University

"**T**his book is a welcome and valuable addition to the destination management literature. It provides an unusually comprehensive and informative overview of critical issues in the field, effectively combining well-crafted discussions of key conceptual and methodological issues with carefully selected and well-presented case studies drawn from a number of contrasting Asian destinations: Thailand, Cambodia, and Singapore. Dr. Jamieson has done an excellent job and produced a book that will be of great value to a wide readership including those directly engaged in destination management as well as those at various levels in academia seeking to broaden their knowledge of the field.

I am particularly impressed by the attention given to issues surrounding applications of GIS and remote sensing, the concise but highly relevant and effective discussion of governance concerns, and the role of festivals and events in community tourism destination management. All of these add a richness and diversity to the book and enhance its value as a source of ideas and guidance on best practice approaches to destination management in developing economies."

Peter Hills, PhD
Professor and Director,
The Centre of Urban Planning
and Environmental Management,
The University of Hong Kong

THHP

The Haworth Hospitality Press®
An Imprint of The Haworth Press, Inc.
New York • London • Oxford

Community Destination Management in Developing Economies

Community Destination Management in Developing Economies

Walter Jamieson
Editor

The Haworth Hospitality Press®
An Imprint of The Haworth Press, Inc.
New York • London • Oxford

For more information on this book or to order, visit
http://www.haworthpress.com/store/product.asp?sku=5140

or call 1-800-HAWORTH (800-429-6784) in the United States and Canada
or (607) 722-5857 outside the United States and Canada

or contact orders@HaworthPress.com

Published by

The Haworth Hospitality Press®, an imprint of The Haworth Press, Inc., 10 Alice Street, Binghamton, NY 13904-1580.

PUBLISHER'S NOTE
The development, preparation, and publication of this work has been undertaken with great care. However, the Publisher, employees, editors, and agents of The Haworth Press are not responsible for any errors contained herein or for consequences that may ensue from use of materials or information contained in this work. The Haworth Press is committed to the dissemination of ideas and information according to the highest standards of intellectual freedom and the free exchange of ideas. Statements made and opinions expressed in this publication do not necessarily reflect the views of the Publisher, Directors, management, or staff of The Haworth Press, Inc., or an endorsement by them.

Cover design by Kerry E. Mack.

Library of Congress Cataloging-in-Publication Data

Community destination management in developing economies / Walter Jamieson, editor.
     p. cm.
   Includes bibliographical references and index.
   ISBN-13: 978-0-7890-2386-5 (hard : alk. paper)
   ISBN-10: 0-7890-2386-5 (hard : alk. paper)
   ISBN-13: 978-0-7890-2387-2 (soft : alk. paper)
   ISBN-10: 0-7890-2387-3 (soft : alk. paper)
   1. Tourism—Developing countries—Management. 2. Hospitality industry—Developing countries—Management. 3. Sustainable development—Developing countries. I. Jamieson, Walter.

G155.D44C66 2006
910'.68—dc22

                                                                    2005020669

CONTENTS

About the Editor

Walter Jamieson, PhD, is Dean of the School of Travel Industry Management, University of Hawaii. Prior to joining the University of Hawaii he was field manager for a Canadian aid project based at the Asian Institute of Technology, Bangkok, where he was also professor of urban environmental management. He has been teaching and working on planning, management, and development issues for thirty years. He has headed major projects in a number of Asian countries and has been responsible for the development of innovative partnerships and collaborative efforts in both public and private sectors. He is a consultant for the United Nations Educational, Scientific, and Cultural Organization (UNESCO) and the United Nations Economic and Social Commission for Asia and the Pacific (UNESCAP) and regularly provides assistance to these organizations. His areas of specific interest and expertise are tourism planning, tourism destination management, strategic environmental management, cultural resource management, knowledge management, and project planning and management. He is currently visiting professor of International Tourism Management, Macau University of Science and Technology and a member of the board of directors of the Pacific Asia Travel Association.

Community Destination Management in Developing Economies
© 2006 by The Haworth Press, Inc. All rights reserved.
doi:10.1300/5140_a

Contributors

Jerome F. Agrusa, PhD, is a professor in the travel industry management program at Hawaii Pacific University. Professor Agrusa received his doctorate in tourism sciences from Texas A&M University and a masters in hospitality management from the Conrad N. Hilton College of Hotel and Restaurant Management at the University of Houston. During his academic career, Dr. Agrusa has published more than 60 referee articles and conference proceedings in the area of tourism and hospitality services. He is well recognized for his research in tourism, and due to his contributions has been invited to be editor in charge of the conference review section of the *Journal of Teaching in Travel and Tourism* and is on the editorial review boards of the *International Journal of Tourism Sciences* and *Asia-Pacific Journal of Tourism Research.* Dr. Agrusa is on the Board of Directors of the Asia-Pacific Tourism Association and the Tourism Research Association–Hawaii Chapter. He has provided consulting services in more than 20 countries, throughout the United States, and to various government and private entities in the hospitality and tourism management industry.

Anthony Chin, PhD, is a professor in the department of economics, faculty of arts and social sciences at the National University of Singapore. He also serves as a principal researcher at the Centre for Transportation Research, faculty of engineering. He has conducted a number of research projects and consultancy works. His research and areas of specialization are on project evaluation of transport and infrastructure projects; urban, housing and location economics; consumer choice and pricing analysis: housing, new and used cars, cell phones, and industrial and commercial property; financing and privatization of infrastructure; demand management and strategic planning of transportation and hub analysis; impact of incentives and disincentives; travel behavior modeling; and economics of crime.

Community Destination Management in Developing Economies
© 2006 by The Haworth Press, Inc. All rights reserved.
doi:10.1300/5140_b

Elizabeth E. Dickson, PhD, P.Biol., is a principal of D & L Associates, an environmental consulting firm dedicated to the use of geographic information systems (GIS) and remote sensing to conduct vegetation and biodiversity assessments and environmental impact assessments (EIAs). Dr. Dickson has a masters in remote sensing from the University of Calgary and a PhD in botany from Cornell University. Dr. Dickson has worked on environmental projects that include the gas pipeline development in the MacKenzie Valley in the Northwest Territories, oilsands development in northern Alberta, and gold exploration in the interior of Alaska. She was a member of a scientific team representing the interests of the Mikisew Cree First Nation that was documented on David Suzuki's *The Nature of Things.*

Panthep Klanarongran currently is secretary general for the Office of the Royal Development Projects Board of Thailand. Following the concepts and theories of His Majesty the King on development, Mr. Klanarongran is responsible for the implementation and management of the King's projects all over the country. He has been working on the royal development projects for a number of years and has extensive experience in community involvement in the King's projects that focused on several areas, including agriculture, environment, public health, occupational promotion, water resources, communication, and public welfare.

Richard M. Levy, PhD, is a professor of planning and urban design at the University of Calgary. He has a bachelor of science in civil engineering from Tufts University, a masters of architecture and PhD in Architecture from the University of California, Berkeley. He currently serves as the coordinator (Chair) for the planning program at the University of Calgary. Since 1996, Dr. Levy has also served as director of computing for the faculty of environmental design. Dr. Levy's research has focused on the use of 3D computer modeling and of geographic information systems (GIS) and computer visualization as decision-making tools in the evaluation of urban development projects in both North America and Asia.

Pallavi Mandke is currently a candidate for a PhD program at Griffith University, Australia. She has been working on urban and environmental issues since 1995. She has been involved in several applied research, demonstration, and community development projects in Asia and has worked with interdisciplinary teams at the local, national, and international levels. Her subject specialization is in urban environmental management and tourism development and planning. In the capacity of a consultant Ms. Mandke has been involved in several consulting assignments for the United Nations Economic and Social Commission for Asia and the Pacific (UNESCAP), Asian Disaster Preparedness Center (ADPC), and Institute for Tourism Studies (IFT).

William A. Ross, PhD, is a professor of environmental science, faculty of environmental design at the University of Calgary. He has been teaching and working on projects related to environmental management issues for a number of years. His main academic interests are in the areas of environmental impact assessment, energy policy, and energy conservation. He is also involved in developing and improving the professional practice of cumulative effects assessment, which is a major issue in environmental impact assessment, as well as in a Canadian International Development Agency (CIDA) funded project offering of an interdisciplinary master's program in energy and the environment in Quito, Ecuador.

Pawinee Sunalai is Southeast Asia training and project coordinator for the School of Travel Industry Management, University of Hawaii. She has an MSc in urban environmental management from the Asian Institute of Technology (AIT). From 1999 to 2002 she has served as a project coordinator for the Canadian Universities Consortium Urban Environmental Management Project funded by Canadian International Development Agency (CIDA). She has been involved in a number of research and demonstration projects and training activities in the areas of tourism, destination management, community-based development, and environmental impact assessment in Thailand, Lao People's Democratic Republic, Cambodia, Vietnam, Taiwan, and Macau.

Geoffrey Wall, PhD, is professor of geography and associate dean for graduate studies and research in the faculty of environmental studies at the University of Waterloo where he is also cross-appointed with the department of recreation and leisure studies. He is also honorary visiting professor at the Metropolitan University, London, and the University of Strathclyde, Glasgow, in the United Kingdom. His research interests focus primarily on aspects of tourism and recreation and secondarily upon the socioeconomic implications of global climate change. He has conducted a number of research projects in these areas in several countries. He has acted as a consultant for international, national, provincial, and local agencies in both the public and private sectors and has written books and numerous articles on tourism and recreation in academic journals. He has also edited a number of volumes on the implications of global climate change.

Willi Zimmermann, PhD, is an associate professor of the School of Management at the Asian Institute of Technology (AIT), Thailand. He currently serves as coordinator of the PHD program for the Swiss-AIT-Vietnam Management Development Programme (SAV) in Vietnam and also is a guest professor at the Guishou Administrative College in China and a senior research fellow, Swiss Federal Institute of Technology Zurich (Institute of Local, Regional and National Planning). Dr. Zimmermann's areas of interest include urban governance with special consideration of sustainability, public sector management, change of environmental policy approaches, policy analysis, and policy implementation.

Preface and Acknowledgments

The development of this book has been an important international initiative. The original motivation for bringing these ideas together came from a Canadian-funded aid project in Southeast Asia concerned with how to better manage community environments. Many of the original concepts were presented at a major international conference, "Sustainable Community Tourism Destination Management," held at the Asian Institute of Technology, November 27 to 29, 2000, in Thailand. Since then the chapters have been updated and new material has been added to ensure the timeliness of the ideas and approaches.

The conference was held under the patronage of Her Royal Highness Princess Maha Chakri Sirindhorn. This was a unique honor since it was the first time a member of the royal family had provided support for a tourism-related event.

We are most grateful to the Canadian International Development Agency for its support. We are also immensely grateful for the support of a significant number of national and international organizations including the Tourism Authority of Thailand, Fine Arts Department of Thailand, Bangkok Metropolitan Administration (BMA), Pacific Asia Travel Association (PATA), Federation of Canadian Municipalities (FCM), Thailand Environment Institute (TEI), World Tourism Organization (WTO), United Nations Environment Programme (UNEP), United Nations Education, Scientific and Cultural Organization (UNESCO), United Nations Economic and Social Commission for Asia and the Pacific (UNESCAP), and World Travel and Tourism Council (WTTC).

This publication brings together a number of leading practitioners who have been actively involved in the actual implementation of sustainable and responsible tourism concepts as they relate to community destination management. It is hoped that the text will help to further encourage discussion on how we can best manage our community tourism destinations responsibly.

Community Destination Management in Developing Economies
© 2006 by The Haworth Press, Inc. All rights reserved.
doi:10.1300/5140_c   *xvii*

Introduction

Tourism as a worldwide phenomenon affects a vast number of people and places and has the potential to touch many more. Hardly a prediction—for international and domestic tourism alike—exists that does not point to overwhelming future growth. With a high and increasing level of tourism activity, communities across the globe must cope with ongoing pressure on their social and cultural systems, infrastructure, services, and environment.

For many destinations tourism is an important source of economic activity. Well-planned and well-managed tourism can create jobs and bring foreign exchange earnings and create opportunities to reduce poverty and gender inequities. In addition, revenues from tourism can be used to improve a destination's infrastructure and provide its residents with a quality of life that would be impossible without the revenues from tourism activity.

However, tourism development can also bring with it significant negative impacts. Among these are the loss of community character and sense of place, environmental degradation, traffic congestion, a shortage of clean water, the inappropriate design of new buildings, significant pressures on a community's infrastructure, the erosion of cultural traditions and values, and an increase in the cost of living.

Tensions will always exist in community destination management. Achieving a balance of positive economic development with the protection, enhancement, and management of the social, cultural, and natural environment of a destination—all important imperatives—will always be a challenge. This task grows ever more complicated with the recognition that a significant number of stakeholders must be included in the decision-making process if the many different issues and factors particular to each destination are to be understood and addressed.

With this challenge as a backdrop, this book brings together a unique group of international authors from a wide range of back-

Community Destination Management in Developing Economies
© 2006 by The Haworth Press, Inc. All rights reserved.
doi:10.1300/5140_01

grounds to discuss innovative approaches that can be used to meet the demands that tourism places on its destinations. Each chapter seeks to move from the rhetoric of sustainable tourism development to practical and grounded solutions.

The book first introduces the concept of community tourism destination management, defines the field, examines the nature of urban and community tourism, and illustrates the management process with examples. It then moves forward to present some key tools and concepts that can be adapted and applied to a wide range of destinations. Finally, a number of multidisciplinary approaches to dealing with various issues within the larger context of tourism destination management are presented, offering practical ideas for readers from various backgrounds concerned with community destination management.

Chapter 1

Defining Urban Tourism Destination Management

Walter Jamieson

Tourism is the world's largest industry, currently providing one out of every ten jobs worldwide. It is also a growing industry; according to the World Tourism Organization's publication "Tourism Highlights: Edition 2003," in 2003 Southeast Asia alone received more than 42 million international tourists—up from 21 million in 1990—and the forecasts are for even larger numbers of domestic and international tourists across the globe. How tourism destinations will cope with these visitor numbers in a sustainable manner is a crucial issue for urban management.

For many Asian cities and countries, tourism development provides much-needed employment and foreign exchange earnings, and in some cases this increased wealth is directed toward the improvement of social and physical conditions for residents. However, tourism can also have negative impacts, and the costs to a local society and its environment can be significant. An influx of tourists and workers from outside a destination can change the local community's social fabric, and development can cause pollution, habitat destruction, and associated health risks. When a tourism destination is managed poorly, as many are, its future as both destination and community is threatened.

Experience has clearly demonstrated that strategic planning and sound management are crucial to the achievement of sustainable development goals. Those responsible for managing destinations need to begin thinking in an integrated manner about the everyday municipal

Community Destination Management in Developing Economies
© 2006 by The Haworth Press, Inc. All rights reserved.
doi:10.1300/5140_02

3

concerns of tourism, and about the cultural and heritage dimensions of a community. At all levels, stakeholders have a common objective: to preserve resources that make a destination unique and appealing to tourists. Sustainable tourism destination management views destinations as more than the sum of their parts and seeks to create destinations that are healthy and viable in the long term for tourists and residents alike.

The sustainable, integrated view of destination management serves to:

- Address the needs of tourists and the economic interests of the tourism industry
- Approach tourism development in a way that reduces the negative impacts
- Protect local people's business interests, heritage, and environment
- Protect the local environment, in part because it is the livelihood of the destination

This chapter provides an overview of the complex web of issues that must be addressed to manage a destination sustainably (Figure 1.1). It does not seek to provide solutions but to identify areas of focus and tools for management that may relate to many different destinations.

WHAT IS SUSTAINABLE TOURISM?

A sustainable approach to tourism destination management is based on globally applicable principles of sustainability. Any steps taken toward the management of a destination should be considered in terms of the values of sustainable development.

Over the past two decades, the interrelatedness of all natural systems and human systems has become abundantly clear. We now understand that no human action ever occurs in total isolation from other natural systems. In other words, we appreciate the reality that humans are dependent on the limited resources of the earth. The global community has been primed for some fundamental changes, which include a search for "sustainable development" based on new modes of resource allocation and accounting, new attitudes toward preservation of environmental integrity, and new ways of making decisions.

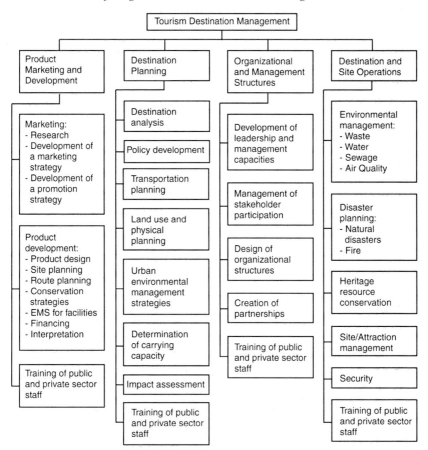

FIGURE 1.1. Factors involved in sustainable tourism destination management.

Among the imperatives that promote and enhance the vision of sustainable futures, including a sustainable future for tourism, are:

- Prudent use of the earth's resources within the limits of the planet's carrying capacity
- Devolution of top-down decision-making responsibilities and capabilities to a broader range of a destination's stakeholders
- The abatement of poverty and gender inequalities, and respect for fundamental human rights

- Enhancement of the quality of life for residents through improved health care, shelter, nutrition, and access to education and income-generating skills
- Preservation of biodiversity and life support systems for all natural habitats
- Preservation of indigenous knowledge and ways of living, and respect for the spiritual and cultural traditions of different peoples

To fulfill these imperatives, governments and other societal agents must struggle to find an appropriate balance between different—and sometimes apparently conflicting—needs and value systems. Whatever the situation, sustainable development must meet three fundamental and equal objectives:

1. *Economic:* production of goods and services (with efficiency as the main consideration)
2. *Environmental:* conservation and prudent management of natural resources (with the preservation of biodiversity and maintenance of ecological integrity as the main considerations)
3. *Social:* the maintenance and enhancement of quality of life (with equity as the main consideration) and intergenerational, as well as intragenerational, equity in the distribution of wealth

Achieving sustainable tourism development requires the private sector and community to act as partners in cooperation toward a sustainable society. Making decisions about sustainable tourism development also requires that communities work within a broad framework, developing decisions that are:

- *Long term:* allowing communities to better anticipate and prevent problems and make risk-reduced decisions
- *Multisectoral:* including the full range of interest and activities in a tourism environment
- *Ecosystem based:* recognizing the cumulative and synergistic effects of all actions on the ecological integrity of a community and region

- *Integrated:* identifying the impact of actions on other sectors, regions, and communities
- *Cognizant:* recognizing the causes and consequences of problems that communities seek to solve, which may involve others and other institutions
- *Full cycle:* thereby understanding the full context of resource use from extraction to end use

If sustainable futures are to be attained, individual tourist resource management decisions must be made with increased understanding of all the dimensions listed. To achieve profitability as well as environmental sustainability in the tourism industry, the industry as a whole must take a different approach to planning and development.

Increasing evidence shows that sustainable tourism requires an integrated approach to tourism planning and management. Only recently has the need to combine the priorities of traditional urban management (transportation, land-use planning, marketing, economic development, fire and safety, etc.) with the necessity of planning for tourism been recognized.

PRINCIPLES OF SUSTAINABLE TOURISM

Some of the most important principles of sustainable tourism development include the following:

- Tourism should be initiated with the help of broad-based community input, and the community should maintain control of tourism development
- Tourism should provide quality employment to its community residents, and linkage between local businesses and tourism should be established
- A code of practice should be established for tourism at all levels— national, regional, and local—based on internationally acceptable standards; and guidelines for tourism operations, impact assessment, monitoring of cumulative impacts, and limits to acceptable change should also be established
- Education and training programs to improve and manage heritage and natural resources should be established

The following chapters demonstrate the range of factors to be considered when managing destinations—and discuss the practical steps that need to be undertaken before a destination can transform a vision of sustainable tourism into a reality. This book should not be considered the only prescription for success, as alternative ways to manage destinations are also available. The process featured in this chapter presents a valuable model when it is paired with initiative and strategic thinking.

PRODUCT MARKETING AND DEVELOPMENT

Product Development

The destination management process requires a destination to develop products—cultural, natural, or intangible in nature—to meet market demands. It is not acceptable simply to assume that "if you build facilities and products, the market will come." Rather, a clear relationship must exist between the nature of the product and the market. This process is more complex than processes associated with other forms of product since tourism planners and managers are often dealing with fragile and irreplaceable resources. The challenge is to achieve a match between product and market. This chapter presents some issues to be addressed in the process of matching product and market.

Product Design

Product is a general term that covers all attractions and services that can be sold to visitors. A destination's product consists of built and natural attractions, tours and packages, services for travelers (e.g., shopping, restaurants, accommodations), and activities. Destinations may choose to concentrate on services such as tour packages, guiding, and interpretation. Natural resources are generally not thought of as products, but an ecotour in a natural park is a product. The heritage architecture of a community is not a product, but its interpretation, through a guided tour, can be seen as a product.

A product-oriented approach to a destination, however, does not mean that only attractions that appeal to tourists, regardless of their appropriateness, should be developed. It means, rather, that the products should be seen as a community's livelihood, and marketed and protected accordingly. Control must be exercised to prevent developments that do not fit the community or cause undesirable effects. Each destination has its own unique product mix, based on its resources, values, needs, and preferences. The result should be an authentic community tourism product attractive to travelers seeking hospitable and unique experiences.

The following elements should be considered when developing a destination's product:

- Choosing authentic themes that reflect local culture(s) and environment and human relationships
- Keeping development in scale with the community and environment
- Ensuring that developments also meet community needs (e.g., through joint use)
- Developing attractions that are attractive and competitive in the long run, not faddish
- Requiring strong community support (rather than imposing new ideas on an unreceptive population)
- Avoiding "parachuting in" ideas that have been successful in other places, since success comes from strong local commitment and enthusiasm
- Choosing themes to position the destination within sustainable development principles
- Considering sports, since many competitions and fun events can be held using existing facilities
- Informing all visitors of tourism plans, goals, and management approach
- Asking local clubs, associations, and businesses to generate meetings and conventions to the extent permitted by infrastructure
- Providing high-quality experiences

Site Planning

To develop attractions and facilities, every destination needs a design plan that takes into consideration issues of visitor management and flow, parking, and access to the attractions. Site designs should be compatible with local heritage and lifestyles to maintain a sense of place and should enhance local architecture and culture.

Site planning refers to the specific location (or sitting) of buildings and related development forms on the land, and considers the functions of buildings, their physical interrelationships, and the characteristics of the natural environmental setting. Site planning also includes the location of roads, parking areas, landscaped and open-space areas, footpaths, and recreational facilities, all of which are integrated with building locations. As is the case at more general levels of planning, an ecological approach to site planning is essential to ensure that developments are well integrated into the natural environment and that environmental problems are not generated. Detailed surveys and analysis of the environmental characteristics of a site are some of the first steps in the site planning process along with determination of specific types, functions, and sizes of buildings and other development forms being planned. This section reviews some of the basic considerations necessary to the site planning of tourist facilities.

Building Relationships

The grouping of buildings (for example, accommodations and their relationships to amenities and recreational facilities) is an important concern of site planning. The type of grouping will depend on the density and character of the development desired, as related to the natural environment.

Types of Development Standards

Several types of specific standards are applicable to the controlled development of tourist facilities. These standards typically include:

- Density of development
- Heights of buildings
- Setbacks of buildings from amenity features, shorelines, roads, lot lines, and other buildings
- Ratio of the building floor area to the site area
- Coverage of the site by buildings and other structures
- Parking requirements
- Other requirements, such as landscaping and open space, public access to amenity features, signs, and utility lines

Design Standards

Design standards should respect the following key elements:

- Local styles and motifs
- Roof lines
- Use of local building materials
- Environmental relationships
- Landscaping design

Designing Tourism Products

Tourism products such as accommodations, hospitality, attractions, events, and other tourist services should be considered in any facility site plan. These tourist facilities include hotels, restaurants, hospitals, and public restrooms. When developing a site plan, the following factors should be considered:

- The scale and type of development. Sustainable development would favor small-scale developments to minimize impacts and encourage incremental (staged) development
- The kind of tourism activities (e.g., ecotourism or heritage tours), facilities, attractions, and amenities to be included in a site plan. Tourism products to be developed will ideally be based on competitive analysis, market research, ecological assessment, and community needs and issues analysis
- Approaches that minimize negative impacts through design, land-use planning, zoning, and management
- Development of project financing strategies that focus on local control and minimize economic leakage from the community
- Tourism vision statements and goals communicated to commercial and other stakeholders of the sites to be included in the planning
- Policies that allow room for future growth and alteration in the plan and sites themselves

Tourists want to visit the main attractions in a destination; therefore, tourist flows through a destination should be established to ensure they are able to see and experience everything they want within a reasonable period of time. Walking tours and promotional material can alert the visitor to the possibilities provided by a site, and can help the visitor avoid those sites not appropriate for tourist use.

Regional route planning can be developed in conjunction with other district or municipal planners, so attractions throughout the region can be developed, creating a broader and more varied tourism experience.

Financing

Financing is a major issue facing those responsible for the management of destinations. Public budgets are often not adequate to cover the rising costs of such basics as the increase of waste disposal to keep up with increasing tourism, the securing of priority for funding for management of historic sites, and the enforcement of building restrictions. Financial sustainability most often involves multiple funding sources with a focus on earned income, and measures that contain operating and restoration costs. Resources for financing include:

- Public sector grants and tax breaks
- Community initiative and investment
- Approaches that stress self-help and self-building
- Joint public/private ventures and partnerships in which often the public sector contributes land or other nonmonetary resources
- Various financing organizations such as nonprofits, trusts, foundations, revolving funds, and community development corporations
- Build-operate-transfer arrangements
- The private sector

Since governments are playing a smaller role in the provision of financing to tourism projects because of limited financial resources, the private sector must supply the majority of financing. These private sources include individuals, banks, trust companies, credit unions, and insurance companies.

Achieving the right funding "mix" by increasing efficiency without compromising the destination's attractiveness is an ongoing issue for many destinations. One possible approach is to combine market economy and public interventions. In this type of financing situation, public authorities are able to retain ownership of resources such as facilities and historic buildings—but the development or renovation responsibility is transferred to private managers. Build-operate-transfer (BOT) procedures are a good example. However, these transfers present other problems. Commercial management is concerned primarily with the facility's ability to attract tourism, which may compromise other considerations, such as its larger role within the destination or conservation concerns. Any attempt at a BOT approach requires the public sector interest group responsible for the facility to be sophisticated in developing management policies and contracts that respect the local community and its environment while providing a reasonable rate of return.

In some situations, it may be inappropriate to contract out the development or management of a particular site. However, supplementary commercial enterprises, such as photography shops or restaurants, can be allowed—and the revenue from these activities can be put toward the ongoing development and protection of the site.

Park and site admission fees, hotel and entertainment taxes, and fund-raising events can also be used to raise money directly for tourism management. A community tourism development corporation can be established to attract investors, identify potential funding sources, and manage funds.

Private corporate sponsorships of events, sites, or even cleanup projects or other public awareness campaigns may be possible. Sponsorships may also be available in the form of expertise or organizational assistance. This type of nonprofit sponsorship is often driven primarily by the desire to improve the sponsor company's image, but as long as the destination's stakeholders retain control over the terms of sponsorship, this type of support has the potential to be beneficial for all concerned.

Donations of aid for specific restoration or preservation projects may also be available from international organizations or foreign governments. However, these are often one-time funds and cannot be depended on in the long term. Often, capital funds are available but operational financing is difficult, if not impossible, to obtain.

Marketing

Attractions change over time, and the level of importance of any attraction over time is affected by two major factors. First, physical characteristics can change: cities may improve or deteriorate in quality, and developed destinations may wear out. Second, market conditions can change. Popularity is as much a function of market forces as physical factors. Influences such as international monetary exchange rates, fashion, personal interests, public policy, and competition can change market segment interest in attractions.

Many factors are within the control of the destination or site manager, whereas others, as previously suggested, result from international or national decisions or from changing consumer behavior. It is vital, therefore, for destinations to understand the motivation and expectation of visitors in order to maintain the viability of the destination. This requires destination managers to have a good understanding of market research and promotion and to maintain a timely database of tourism trends and the ability of their site to meet visitor expectations.

This chapter should not be seen as a primer on marketing but simply as a series of suggestions to be considered when developing a destination's marketing approaches.

Marketing for Sustainability

Whereas traditional marketing places heavy emphasis on the potential customer's needs and desires, sustainable tourism marketing begins with the consideration of a community's values, goals, and needs. Preservation of the integrity of the natural and cultural resource base is the foundation of such an approach. But attention must also be given to ensuring that the destination's tourism industry is competitive and economically sustainable, and that the community will continue to support tourism and the changes it often brings.

Tourists are not always interested in the host culture or its environment. Not all forms of tourism or types of visitor are compatible with local goals and conditions. Careful attention to high-quality, high-yield visitors will benefit the community much more than indiscriminate mass marketing.

For the most part, mass tourism is incompatible with a sustainable tourism marketing strategy. We can define *mass tourism* as being large in scale and oriented toward the widest possible range of customers. Many destinations are quite successfully pursuing mass tourism. However, the cost is high, and negative impacts can easily outweigh the benefits, at least from the residents' perspective. Furthermore, once set in motion, it is difficult or impossible to reverse the process of mass tourism development. It will result in external, rather than local, control, and often local businesses and residents will be pushed aside.

The alternative strategy is niche marketing, or the pursuit of market segments that will meet the community's sustainable tourism goals. Most people can be attracted to a popular beach resort because of the universal appeal of sun, sea, and sand, but not everyone is particularly interested in bird-watching, local festivals, or homestays. The more focused marketing efforts are, the more control can be retained over the process.

At times, it has been argued that the tourism industry needs constant growth, and that maximum amounts of promotion are required to sustain profits and jobs. This is simply not the case. Mass marketing sows the seeds of its own problems—namely the "boom and bust" cycle that typically results when high levels of demand lead to oversupply, which then results in low levels of use and inefficient operations. From the destination's, and especially the residents', point of view, it is far better to concentrate on a single or a few prime segments and avoid the pitfalls of mass marketing. Furthermore, much less development and servicing is required if year-round occupancy/use can be assured, rather than the constant building of new infrastructure to cater to growing peak-season demand.

A sustainable approach to tourism marketing still requires good market research, detailed segmentation to find the best target markets, attention to customer needs and preferences, and delivery of high-quality products and services. The difference between a sustainable and a standard approach is that sustainable marketing favors the community and its environment: industry and community must be in partnership to agree on the goals and process.

Marketing for sustainable tourism involves the same processes and elements used by all businesses and destinations, but the orientation is quite different. Sustainable tourism marketing stresses the following:

- Meeting the needs and goals of the community
- Matching locally supported products to appropriate segments
- Attracting high-yield and high-quality visitors, not large numbers
- Cultivating the right image to convey environmentally and culturally sensitive messages by employing unique selling propositions

- Communicating effectively with, and educating, all visitors
- Employing environmental and cultural interpretation
- Managing the visitor and encouraging the adoption of codes of conduct
- Achieving efficiency by avoiding high peaks of demand and overuse
- Offering high-quality attractions and services
- Researching appropriate segments, communication effectiveness, and resultant impacts
- Building repeat trade

Market Research

Market research has a number of important aims:

- Understanding what existing and potential visitors want in terms of benefits and experiences, products, and services
- Identifying the appropriate target market segments
- Matching products to potential market segments
- Keeping track of what the competition is doing
- Understanding the relative importance of all elements in the marketing mix (e.g., how important is price?)

In marketing, the key is always to focus on what potential customers want, need, and will demand. If a destination wishes to develop ecotourism, two questions must be addressed: (1) Who will purchase ecotours? and (2) Will demand be sufficient to justify the investment? Niche marketing requires that very careful attention be given to measuring potential demand from target segments and finding ways of reaching them effectively.

Market potential can be evaluated in several ways. The starting point is basic research into tourism trends; usually government agencies, industry associations, and educational institutions can provide this data. It is more difficult, however, to obtain demand-related information specific to certain areas, communities, or businesses. In these cases, original market research is likely to become necessary.

Many good ideas fail because of the mistaken assumption that demand naturally follows supply. It is not sufficient to know that demand for a product or experience exists. It must be shown, through research and a feasibility study, that the proposed development can capture an adequate share of the market. It is always important to keep in mind that a great deal of competition exists for the consumer's attention, time, and money.

Since demand will come from specific segments of the global marketplace, segmentation and selection of target markets are crucial parts of this process. Because sustainable tourism marketing is the opposite of mass marketing, extra care must be taken to identify and attract appropriate market segments.

Development of a Marketing Strategy

A summary of the research and analysis undertaken should be included in the actual marketing plan. Goals and objectives should be clearly stated, strategies articulated, and an action plan and budget outlined. The marketing plan is usually revised annually in light of ongoing research and evaluation of its effectiveness. It should incorporate a multiyear strategy for each element of the marketing mix, since few strategies can be fully implemented in one year.

The following is an outline of a typical marketing plan for a destination marketing organization:

- Vision and goals for the destination
- General marketing goals
- Situation analysis and market research
- Resource and supply appraisal
- Market potential
- Strategies, goals, and objectives
- Action plan and budget
- Evaluation of key performance criteria

Monitoring, Evaluation, and Revisions

Every marketing planning process requires the ongoing monitoring of results and constant attention to improvements. Monitoring usually requires specific research efforts and the establishment of indicators. The types of research necessary are indicated in the following, with comments on sustainability requirements.

- *Tracking studies:* To determine the effectiveness and efficiency of marketing, the awareness levels, attitudes, travel patterns, and satisfaction levels of both visitors and target segments must be tracked over time.
- *Impact assessment:* To measure concrete and qualitative results from marketing efforts in particular, and tourism in general, including economic, social, cultural, and environmental effects.
- *Measuring costs and benefits:* Statistics can be obtained from tourism activity.

The ultimate evaluation consists of decisions about tourism goals and strategies in general. These issues include setting limits, monitoring changing target market segments, and modifying the marketing mix. The issues obviously affect the entire community development strategy and all of its management systems.

Development of a Promotion Strategy

Image-making is an essential part of sustainable tourism marketing. The sustainable tourism destination wants to portray itself using attractive symbols and messages. On the other hand, the words "green," "ecotourism," and "environmentally friendly" have often been abused, so clichés must be avoided. Most often, the best approach stresses authenticity, exclusivity, uniqueness, and sound visitor management practices. The focus should be on image-making for precise targets.

From a sustainability point of view, a number of factors must be considered:

- Promotion must be targeted and fully informative, otherwise false expectations will be generated.
- Quality tourists are informed tourists.
- Quality products are marketed differently from mass tourism products (for example, value is more important than price).
- Information and interpretation are also important elements in the travel experience.

Conclusion

In this chapter, only the basic points to be considered in any marketing development process are identified. It is vital that destinations work with professionals when developing market strategies and conducting research to ensure their competitiveness in the global market while respecting their sustainable development goals.

DESTINATION PLANNING

The intricacy of the tourism system is demonstrated by the variety of individuals and groups that can affect a destination's future. This complexity makes destination planning vital but also difficult. Clearly, cooperative and proactive direction is needed to guide planning and development. This chapter will identify actions required for the development and implementation of effective sustainable tourism strategies. The process can be described as dynamic, participative, and adaptable to the needs and concerns of a destination's many stakeholders.

No formula exists for the amount of planning a particular situation calls for, and clearly each societal context will determine what is appropriate. Similarly, although sustainable tourism calls for a high level of local involvement with tourism planning and development, the amount and quality of resident participation will vary depending on cultural and political factors at the destination. It is obviously not very useful to develop a sophisticated planning system if it has no political or community support. In these cases, one might first have to generate an appropriate setting or structure for a planning process.

A strategic planning approach, whereby the disparate planning and development activities related to tourism are linked to an overall broad strategic plan to provide an integrated framework for directing tourism, is essential for sustainable tourism. Strategic planning seeks an optimal fit between the system and its environment. Hence, it achieves the following:

- Maintains a long-term perspective
- Creates a vision
- Specifies goals as well as the specific actions and resources necessary to achieve these goals
- Remains dynamic, flexible, and adaptable
- Ensures that formulation and implementation of the strategic plan are closely linked through constant monitoring, environmental scanning, evaluation, and adjustment

- Ensures close coordination between local and regional legislative and political structures
- Requires community participation and support
- Is supported by an informed, educated, and aware community
- Includes an innovative and inclusive organizational structure for joint planning
- Applies the principles of sustainable tourism development to ensure the long-term sustainability of the ecology, local economy, and the sociocultural values of the community while distributing benefits equitably among the stakeholders

Many approaches to planning can be taken, from no planning at all to a centralized, top-down method, but all good planning generally contains the following elements and action steps:

- Defining a vision and mission statement
- Implementing a situational analysis
- Developing strategic goals
- Evaluating strategic alternatives to achieving these goals
- Developing strategies
- Implementing strategies that include measurable objectives and detailed action plans
- Monitoring and evaluating strategies and action plans
- Adjusting strategic and operational plans, based on information and feedback from evaluation and constant scanning of the external environment

Destination Analysis

Once the community has decided it is receptive to tourism, it is important to conduct a destination analysis to assess the community's infrastructure and tourism resources. Carrying out this task in a comprehensive manner can benefit everyone. The objectives of this process include the following:

- To determine what the destination possesses in terms of tourism attractions
- To determine the location of tourism resources, infrastructure, and attractions
- To assess the tourism qualities of resources and attractions

- To determine what stage of readiness for tourism the attractions and resources are in
- To develop some initial priorities
- To outline an action plan

The nature of a community's tourism resources is illustrated in Figure 1.2. In addition, each community has significant infrastructure concerns that must be stressed. These factors are illustrated in Figure 1.3. Tourism infrastructure is essential to a determination of the destination's readiness for tourism. The assessment process can examine a number of factors, as illustrated in Figure 1.4. The primary tourism infrastructure is supported by a range of other factors, all of which are crucial to determine success and help the community achieve the highest possible economic return from tourism. These factors are illustrated in Figure 1.5.

Policy Development

In order to make plans in accordance with sustainable guidelines, a destination needs to develop a policy that reflects all stakeholders' concerns and objectives. Developing this policy can be a long and complex process because of the different and often competing interests of diverse groups that make up the stakeholders in any destination.

Even if it is not a binding document, a community-formed policy can be used by constituents to demonstrate to elected politicians the desires and goals of the community. This document may be particularly useful during transitions of public leadership at election time,

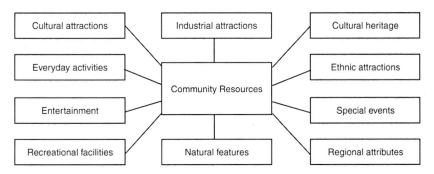

FIGURE 1.2. Community tourism resources.

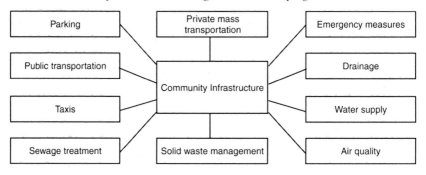

FIGURE 1.3. Community infrastructure.

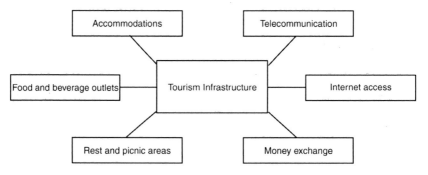

FIGURE 1.4. Tourism infrastructure.

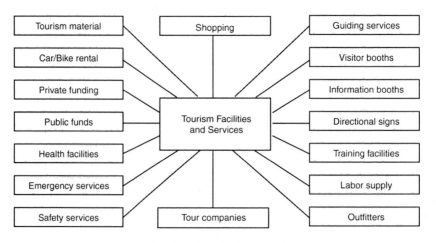

FIGURE 1.5. Tourism facilities and service.

whereby potential incumbents can be asked to make a commitment to the vision statement. Use of a community policy as a relevant implementation tool requires the support of local government, stakeholders, and businesses. The policy also needs to fit well with regional, national, and global tourism policies. Potential for conflict exists in this area, as top-down planners often support different tourism development priorities than local stakeholders do. Destinations must determine what can be done locally and what requires regional and national government assistance. They must ensure new political and legislative structures and establish sustainable tourism development frameworks.

Public Participation

Managing tourism in a sustainable way requires that everyone affected by tourism be informed and involved in tourism—both in the planning process and the implementation of policies and action plans. Local people can be involved in tourism to varying degrees, ranging from information gathering to ownership, direct decision making, and employment in planning, project development, and service delivery. In the context of sustainable tourism development, a clear distinction has to be made between consultation and participation. Although community consultation is highly recommended, it is not synonymous with participation. Sustainable tourism development requires participation that allows people the right to order and influence their world. To accomplish this, opportunities must be created that enable community members to participate as fully as possible in directing the development of their community.

Local citizenry can get involved in the tourism planning process directly (for instance, via committees and workshops), or indirectly, through public meetings, surveys, etc. Direct participation in tourism-related projects is also highly recommended, since this creates a sense of ownership in the outcome of the process. Participation may also allow the benefits of tourism to be distributed more widely among community members, both directly and indirectly. More direct local involvement in decision making, for example, may enable residents to request a specific portion of tax benefits from tourism to be allocated toward community development and the protection of the tourism resource base.

Determination of Carrying Capacity

In its simplest form, carrying capacity measures the sustainable level of destination use. In fact, determination of carrying capacity is a complex process, particularly when a range of products and services must come from the same environment (as in the case of tourism). Yet the question remains the same: how many tourists/visitors can be accommodated in a destination, and within specific portions of the destination, without threatening the long-term sustainability of a specific site?

The concept of carrying capacity has value particularly because it draws attention to limits and thresholds beyond which a site does not wish to tread. But realistically, the following factors need to be considered:

- Tourism depends on many attributes of an environment, among them aesthetic qualities, maintenance of wildlife, access to shoreline, and/or ability to support active uses. Each of these attributes has its own response to different levels of use.
- The impact of human activity on a system may be gradual and affect different parts of the system at different rates. Whereas some environmental resources may be highly sensitive to human impact (e.g., habitats for fragile or endangered species), others degrade gradually in response to different levels of use.
- Every environment serves multiple purposes, and its sensitivity to different use levels depends on the values of all users.
- Different types of use have different impacts.
- Tourism managers need measurable guidelines to reduce the risk that they will unknowingly step over biological or cultural thresholds and degrade the product, cause other adverse effects, or discourage customers.

The success of the tourism planning effort depends greatly on the ability of a destination to monitor the implementation of action plans, to achieve its objectives, and to set and monitor critical indicators and carrying-capacity thresholds related to the resources being used. Carrying capacity, in this context, refers to the amount of use or impact a resource can handle without its health or survival being seriously affected. Indicators and thresholds need to be established that provide decision makers with information enabling them to evaluate, and make timely decisions regarding, changes caused by tourism. The concept of carrying capacity is fully discussed in Chapter 9.

Conclusion

Many tools and concepts are available in the destination planning process. In this chapter only a few of these have been indicated, but it is recommended that all available tourism destination planning advice and support be used to ensure long-term sustainability.

ORGANIZATIONAL STRUCTURE AND MANAGEMENT

Establishing the right organizational and management structure is often the key to success. Each situation requires a distinct organizational structure, but the importance of stakeholder involvement cannot be overemphasized. Generally speaking, every destination needs a structure for the management of tourism and its many related issues.

Design of Organizational Structures

The establishment of ongoing leadership will facilitate future planning-related actions, such as constant scanning of the environment and the identification of opportunities and management problems as they emerge, thereby increasing the ability to develop sustainable tourism. Some pros and cons of a few leadership bodies are outlined in Table 1.1.

Regardless of the structure of the existing or newly created organization, some major areas of responsibility can be the following:

- Participation in community tourism strategy planning
- Guiding and evaluation of physical development, programs, and activities
- Ongoing monitoring of tourism development and impacts
- Guiding impact mitigation and adjusting tourism strategies

- Making sure that sustainable tourism practices are implemented, including economic incentives for local ownership and local control of tourism, education and training of locals to participate in the tourism industry, and equitable access for residents to tourism facilities and activities
- Establishment of subcommittees for management of various aspects of the overall tourism strategy
- Assistance with ongoing community education and awareness of tourism activities

TABLE 1.1. Some advantages of different leadership bodies.

Organizations	Roles	Advantages
Convention and visitors bureau/local destination management organization	Tourism marketing and promotion, visitor information services.	May be funded by public and/or private sources, hence may have funding sources. Cons: Narrow functional area.
Chamber of commerce	Business development, networking, support.	Familiarity with broad business community needs and functions. Cons: May have pro-development philosophy.
Local council/economic development office	Economic development, resource allocations, public services.	Legitimate representative of community, has potential funding source.
Community group (e.g., resident or environmental organization)	Advocacy, lobby group, networking.	Representative of local resident interests. Cons: Generally volunteer based, hence may lack funding or suffer volunteer burnout.
Community tourism organization	Strategic tourism planning and management, ongoing monitoring of impacts and planning outcomes, adjustment of overall strategic plan as required.	Broad-based community interests represented with active guidance or tourism. Cons: May be time consuming to set up and may be costly to maintain, depending on activity.

Creation of Partnerships

One of the most important lessons acknowledged in all areas of development is that partnerships greatly influence the success of any initiative. Public/private partnerships among government, public organizations, community organizations, industry, and commerce are seen as the cornerstone of success in many destination initiatives. Partnerships can bring together many different sets of ideas, points of view, and contributions of various kinds, whether financial, social, or political in nature, that help to achieve a successful heritage area strategy.

Conflict Management

Managing the objectives and opinions of stakeholders is critical for tourism organizations involved in development. Controversy can be harmful to tourism proposals. Lengthy delays may ensue, adverse media attention could harm the image or reputation of the developer, and community resistance to proposals (due to perceived threats of negative impacts) can make it difficult for developers to establish a mutually beneficial working relationship in the destination. Although a detailed treatment of this vital issue of conflict management is not possible in this manual, the following points provide some useful direction.

- Anticipate and prevent conflicts where possible.
- Establish mechanisms that enable effective communication, consultation, and participation of stakeholders in development decision making.
- Investigate community values and attitudes and involve the community (through consultation and more direct participation) prior to making commitments on issues that can have a significant impact on the community and environment.
- Identify and involve key stakeholders in the conflict management and conflict resolution processes.
- When it comes to dealing with the local community, it is better to be as inclusive as possible. Recognize, however, that this will require the management of a diversity of opinions, interests, attitudes, and values of stakeholders who have varying knowledge

and communication skills. The participation mechanisms developed must deal with these challenges. Different situations may require different mechanisms.

In addition, ensure that certain stakeholders who are involved in conflict management/resolution have the information necessary to make informed decisions and give opinions in a timely manner. It is also important to make the information comprehensible to everyone. Understanding of the issues should not be compromised because of unduly technical jargon.

Training of Public and Private Sector Staff

Proper training ensures that local people are involved in the actual implementation and management of tourism in the community. Their involvement reduces leakage of revenue, enables import substitution, and generates employment.

Sustainable tourism development requires the establishment of education and training programs to improve public understanding and enhance business, vocational, and professional skills. Training should include courses in tourism, hotel management, and other relevant topics, and can be developed through linkages with area and regional educational institutions such as community colleges or universities.

The training of staff to be knowledgeable about tourists' needs and views and about the destination itself is important in any situation in which an interaction between visitors and staff will occur. This requires an investment of time and resources that is often difficult to justify in a restricted budget situation, but training dimensions cannot be neglected if the site is to be protected and the message transmitted to the visitor.

It is important to note that training and education can take many forms, ranging from formal, in-class instruction and distance education to self-paced, computer-based learning and publications or manuals.

Achieving the right kind of organizational structure and management is essential if a destination is to achieve a sustainable future. Many different approaches to creating a management structure are available, but the principles identified previously are important dimensions of any organizational structure. The most important consideration is that all stakeholders from the community, public, and private sectors must be seen as essential actors in the overall management of the tourism destination.

DESTINATION SITE MANAGEMENT/OPERATIONS

Once destinations have developed policies, plans, and management structures, they will need to develop management operation policies and procedures to maintain the ongoing attractiveness of the destination and ensure protection of local cultures and environments. This control should not be seen solely as the responsibility of local authorities, but rather should involve cooperation of all stakeholders in the community.

Environmental Management

A major task for any destination is to improve the urban environment, both within the destination itself and in its immediate surroundings. This is a topic for significant further discussion, but certainly any ongoing management of tourism destinations must take into account the following physical factors:

- Roads
- Drainage
- Water supply
- Electric power
- Sewage disposal
- Solid waste disposal
- Telecommunications
- Sanitation and public health standards

Urban Environmental Management for Facilities

Part of developing a destination's product is ensuring that sustainable values are held throughout the tourism industry. An environmental management system (EMS) is a system that assists facilities, such as hotels and restaurants, in the improvement of their overall environmental performance. The EMS takes a holistic approach to the facility, monitoring its environmental behavior from the beginning of the process (e.g., inflow of resources and products into the facility) through to the end. This system monitors all environmentally sensitive areas, such as solid waste generation, consumption of water, disposal of wastewater, and consumption of energy (electricity and other fuels).

Heritage Resource Conservation

As mentioned earlier, a destination's historic, cultural, and natural heritages are often its main attractions. These resources must be protected accordingly, and management approaches need to make their conservation a priority. Conservation in a destination demands a systematic approach and requires discipline. Historic sites have technical conservation issues too specific for discussion in this chapter, but a conservation plan to address the detailed needs of any destination should be drafted during the planning phase of tourism development. The issue of heritage conservation is discussed fully in Chapter 12.

Site/Attraction Management

One of the major management tasks on any site is to deal with visitor numbers, behavior, and impacts. As discussed earlier, every site has its use limits. When those limits are exceeded, damage begins to accumulate, and visitor experience is compromised. Visitor impact, therefore, is the combined effect of the number of people using a site, the type of activity at the site, the timing of visits, and the ability of particular environments to withstand use.

Management of site use might be fairly straightforward if it were not for the need to balance visitor volumes with the positive economic impact generated from those volumes. An ideal level of use might be incompatible with an attempt to meet the economic objectives of a site. It is the responsibility of the site management team to attempt to ensure the least possible damage to the site while guaranteeing its financial viability.

Managing Visitors

If the site is to maintain its financial viability and protect its integrity, an ongoing effort must be made to understand visitors and their expectations. This can be accomplished in several ways.

A number of possible strategies for managing visitor numbers can be used. It is possible simply to reduce the number of visitors to a site, reduce the number of people at any one time, or limit the number of people in a particular place. Softer techniques, such as helping to change visitor behavior through education, can be implemented as well. Physical strategies can also be used to make the site more resistant to change. Typically, in any situation, all of these strategies must coalesce in a management plan. Some management strategies appropriate to any of these approaches include the following:

- Restricting or limiting entry to the area
- Reducing numbers of large groups
- Implementing a quota system
- Using pricing techniques to reduce demand
- Directing visitors to other areas
- Having different pricing policies for different times of the week and year
- Developing a reservations system
- Using a system of lotteries to determine who can use a site
- Extending hours at particularly busy times of the year
- Limiting accommodations near the site

Each of these management strategies brings with it certain costs and benefits and has important political realities that must be reconciled as part of the management process.

Managing the Site and the Surrounding Environment

No one site exists on its own, and many depend on the surrounding community for financial and social support. In addition, the surrounding community most often provides a wide range of visitor services and attractions that are essential to the full visitor experience. The site management plan must also consider how to manage the relationship between the site itself and the surrounding community. It is useful to think of the community in its many dimensions as one of the many stakeholders involved in overall site management. Various forms of participation are possible, but it is essential that the relationship with the surrounding community be well thought out and incorporated into any planning and management exercise.

Individual sites and attractions need to consider not only the surrounding community but other sites and attractions, nearby and regionally. Often, a heritage site is not viable on its own and must work closely with other tourist attractions in the immediate vicinity to collectively provide a more robust tourist destination. If a group of sites, or even a group of destinations, work together to each establish a unique regional niche, visitors will likely stay longer in the area and visit each destination or site for a different experience. However, independent efforts in areas such as marketing could undermine the tourism potential of a region and result in a duplication of effort and a waste of resources.

Visitors Amenities and Services

Once visitors arrive at the site or destination, they must be treated in the best possible manner to ensure their satisfaction, willingness to return, and recommend the site to others. Site services and amenities can range from simple provisions, such as drinking fountains and benches, to a well-cared-for environment.

Visitor amenities and services exist both on- and off-site. On-site amenities and services can include the following:

• Drinking water
• Toilets
• Public telephones
• Postal services
• Emergency medical services
• Garbage removal and disposal

The range of on-site amenities is obviously a function of the scale of the site. Larger sites can offer a full range of eating and accommodation services. If these services are contracted out, leasing and contract administration will be necessary.

Off-site amenities can include:

• Accommodations of various kinds
• Restaurants
• Retail activities
• Services, such as car repair and e-mail
• Recreational facilities

- Entertainment possibilities
- Health care

Although site managers do not control these amenities, they can influence community and regional private sector interests to provide some of them through their public relations programs.

Safety and Security

Since the Bali bombings of 2002, tourism in Asia has encountered a significant number of disasters. Among many other disasters, severe acute respiratory syndrome (SARS), bird flu, the tsunami of 2004, and the most recent bombings of Bali in 2005 have occurred. Impacts of September 11 and the Iraq war have been felt globally as well. Although these events have had a temporary impact on tourism numbers, the region has shown a considerable ability to respond after each of the disasters, and overall tourism in the region has remained constant and in some regions is growing. Certain locations continue to be impacted by some of these disasters, but overall tourism is doing better than expected. One of the lessons is that destinations must ensure that safety and security are an integral part of their planning and operations.

No matter what the destination, most tourists want to feel secure, not only from theft and crime but in the abilities of the destination to deal with any problem that may arise. It is often more a sense of security, rather than anything tangible, that tourists are seeking.

A destination's fire, police, and hospital facilities are paramount. This includes, for example, doctors or police who can speak the tourist's language and are trustworthy and sympathetic. If problems do arise for tourists, a lack of preparation on the part of the destination will make it seem decidedly less tourist-friendly.

When visiting a foreign or even a domestic destination, tourists want to feel confident that the water they are drinking is safe and that the food is free of disease. Strategies to promote these feelings of security revolve around training and awareness campaigns for locals. For example, hotel and restaurant workers may need training about what tourists find acceptable and unacceptable in terms of hygiene and food preparation. The most important strategy, however, is to communicate with tourists. The unknown is frightening; honest, straightforward information will reassure them about what is and is not safe in a destination. For example, if tap water is not safe to drink but is safe for brushing teeth, explain to visitors why, and direct them to a place where they can purchase bottled water. Many tourists to Asia worry about malaria. If malaria prophylactics are necessary, it is important to make tourists aware of this before they arrive and to reassure them that the destination is able to cope with any potential problems.

Disaster Planning

The Southeast Asia region is prone to major disasters such as fires, typhoons, and particularly floods. Destinations should be concerned about the impact of disasters, not only for the safety of local people but also because a destination's ability to deal with the situation effectively and professionally is important in terms of tourists' perceptions of safety. Disaster planning is crucial; the destination must be prepared to deal with most possible eventualities.

Limitations exist for traditional top-down, relief-based disaster management. During times of disaster, local governments are in the best position to provide leadership, supervise the distribution of relief goods and medicine, and manage evacuations. Since local governments have the most at stake and are the most closely involved in local development, they can be effective in planning long-term risk reduction.

Natural disasters can turn into public relations disasters as well. If word gets out in the media and is communicated to the destination's target markets, tourists will be afraid to visit. Public relations "damage control" is of the utmost importance in mitigating a disaster's negative effects on the tourism industry. For example, if a typhoon hits one corner of an island and images of the damage reach the international press, the destination must work hard to publicize that only one portion of the island has been affected and the rest is open for business as usual.

A destination must also be physically prepared to respond to emergencies. Disaster planning should consider how to preserve the resources themselves along with the well-being of the host community and guests. Disasters can destroy both natural and cultural heritage. A good disaster plan can reduce the impact on heritage and natural resources and minimize damage. For example, if a fire occurs, are local fire brigades trained to salvage ancient paintings from a burning museum?

Considerations of water, transport, and communication in times of crisis are internal dimensions that must be planned ahead of time and cannot be managed by a damage control public relations team.

CONCLUSION

Although most tourism planners and destination managers recognize the global nature of tourism, events that have occurred both within and outside the region have demonstrated the importance of thinking globally and in an integrated way. It is no longer possible to accept the traditional tourism model that has existed in which certainty and growth—with minor blips—are business as usual. A realization that uncertainty and crisis will be an integral aspect of the management and planning of destinations now exists. Globalization has also brought with it the need to be ever more cognizant of the competitive nature of travel and tourism and the need to regard product development and promotion as essential components of the management process. Finally, conservation and enhancement of the cultural and natural environment are increasingly seen as important reasons why people will travel to Asia. This chapter has attempted to provide an introduction to these various dimensions of the management process. Many of these issues are further discussed in the following chapters in order to provide a fuller understanding of the management process.

Chapter 2

The Nature of Urban
and Community Tourism

Geoffrey Wall

THE IMPORTANCE OF TOURISM

Although tourism has a long history, it grew most rapidly in the last half of the twentieth century following World War II, and it continues to grow. Successive transportation improvements, particularly the creation of wide-bodied jets that have enabled people to travel faster, farther, and relatively cheaply, have paved the way for the proliferation of package tours to international destinations—making travel accessible to greater numbers of people. International tourism is still beyond the reach of many of the poor of the developing world, who are more likely to be workers in the tourism industry than tourists themselves. It has, however, become an integral part of the lives of many in the Western world, and is becoming increasingly accessible to growing middle classes elsewhere. In fact, growth in international tourism has shown considerable persistence; wars and economic crises have proven to be only temporary setbacks in a phenomenon that continues to increase steadily.

Massive infrastructure and a variety of organizations have been developed to cater to the needs and wants of travelers. Although tourism is discretionary, it is supported by businesses of varying types and scales, which would not exist without tourism. These businesses collectively employ an immense number of people with a variety of skill levels.

Community Destination Management in Developing Economies
© 2006 by The Haworth Press, Inc. All rights reserved.
doi:10.1300/5140_03

With respect to arrivals and departures, international tourism continues to be dominated by Western Europe. This is a result of the relatively high standards of living and commensurately high discretionary incomes, legislated holidays for workers, and the large number of countries clustered in close proximity, which makes it relatively easy to cross an international border and thus be considered an international traveler. The fastest rates of travel growth are being experienced in other places, such as the Middle East, but these figures describe the movement of relatively few people. Among the world regions with substantial tourism flows, the fastest growth rates have occurred in Southeast Asia. Growth has been notable particularly within the regional market as the growing urban middle classes have taken the opportunity to visit other countries in the region and, indeed, to travel farther. The so-called Asian economic crisis has shown itself to be only a temporary setback, and an upward trend in the region is once again evident.

Many countries in Southeast Asia have prioritized tourism in their development strategies. They have eased travel formalities and increased marketing budgets, which include the designation of special "travel years" to attract inbound customers. They have developed national tourism plans and have encouraged investors to augment their infrastructure through tax allowances and other economic incentives. They have succeeded; tourism is now a major source of both foreign investment and foreign currency earnings in most countries in the region.

However, tourism phenomena are not evenly distributed globally, regionally, or nationally. They are highly concentrated in specific locations, especially in parts of capital cities and areas such as Phuket and Pattaya in Thailand and Bali in Indonesia, which have become internationally renowned tourism resort destinations. After the October 2002 bombings, Bali had begun to slowly recover when the destination was hit again in October 2005. All indications prior to the October 2005 bombings were that the destination was going to return to pre–October 2002 arrival figures. At the time of writing it is difficult to predict what the impact of the 2005 bombings will be. Recovery in Phuket has been somewhat more successful after the tsunami in 2004, but all predictions are that it may be several years before visitor arrival numbers will reach pre-tsunami figures. The situation in Phuket is complicated by the number of bodies that have not yet been recovered, which causes concern among certain tourism groups from Asia. These two incidents have demonstrated the fragility of tourism against forces outside the power of the community or region that affect the overall success and sustainability of a destination. Therefore, somewhat paradoxically, tourism is a global phenomenon, yet it is still highly concentrated in specific locations. It is in these locations that most of the positive and negative impacts of tourism occur.

Tourism is a potent economic force at both global and local levels, involving substantial flows of investment and expenditures. It also requires large movements of goods and services from one location to another—ranging from whiskey, steak, furniture, and refrigeration equipment to advanced transportation and telecommunication systems. It involves massive modification of environments as transportation termini, networks, accommodations, and attractions are built to attract and cater to visitors. It also requires the movement and interaction of people who have very different backgrounds, religions, lifestyles, and standards of living—some at play, others at work. The relationships between them may be fleeting, managed by culture brokers such as tour guides and books, and uneven in power relations, having different meanings for hosts and guests, visitors and those visited, and businesses and clients. Images are sent across the world in an attempt to attract more people, and these images are confirmed or modified through brief, real experiences. They are further propagated as visitors return home with photographs and souvenirs, contributing to the identities of those who have returned as well as those who continue to toil in the destination areas, with accompanying implications for self-worth, self-discovery, and status.

Although sometimes regarded as fun and frivolous, tourism is in fact a major agent of global change both economically and environmentally, and because of its personal and psychological effects on both visitors and residents.

THE NATURE OF TOURISM

Tourism has been defined by Mathieson and Wall (1982) as the temporary movement of persons to destinations outside the normal home and workplace, the activities undertaken during the stay, and the facilities created to cater for the needs of tourists.

Although this broad definition provides an overview of some aspects of tourism, it is less helpful in providing guidelines for the collection of information to facilitate the analysis of tourism phenomena. For this purpose, two main perspectives have been adopted: demand-side and supply-side. Each will be considered in turn.

Demand-side definitions approach tourism from the perspective of the tourist and determine the importance of tourism according to the number of tourists who participate. However, this approach is less straight forward than it might seem at first glance. Four issues must be resolved before a person can be considered a tourist. They include the following:

1. *Motivation:* Are all travelers tourists, or only some? Are tourists only pleasure travelers, or should business travelers be included? What about trips based on multiple motivations?
2. *Spatial component:* How far must people travel, or what kind of border must they cross to be considered a tourist? For international travel, an international border must be crossed. For domestic travel, this definition is less straightforward.
3. *Temporal component:* How long must a person stay away from home to be considered a tourist? Many definitions require that they stay at least one night, but this may be inappropriate for many day-trip destinations. However, if individuals stay longer than a year, they then become migrants.
4. *Transport:* This is not often a major issue except in specific situations. For example, in the case of passengers on cruise ships, it may be desirable to regard them as tourists (excursionists) even though they may not stay overnight.

Much has been published about the definition and categorization of tourists. The United Nations and the World Tourism Organization have suggested guidelines for data collection. However, these guidelines may need to be modified in specific circumstances, and a consequent lack of comparability exists between studies.

Beyond the problem of definition, other issues concerning demand-side tourism need to be addressed. Most industries are not defined on the basis of their consumers, i.e., on the numbers and characteristics of people who purchase their products. For example, agriculture is not defined according to people who eat food, and the automobile industry is not usually measured through calculations of the number and nature of people who drive cars, although this information may be useful for marketing purposes. Rather, such industries are usually assessed according to the number of employees and the value of their output. Demand-side data on tourism cannot be readily compared with data from most other economic sectors. As a result, the relative importance of tourism cannot be assessed, and the great social and economic significance of tourism remains unrecognized.

Faced with this situation, attempts have been made to measure tourism from a supply-side perspective, according to the number and types of businesses that cater to the needs of tourists. However, this is more easily said than done. Hotels, restaurants and transportation systems that cater primarily to tourists may also have a local, nontourist clientele. Others, such as taxis and laundries, may have a mixed clientele. Furthermore, some operations with a large tourism clientele, such as museums and parks, may regard themselves as only marginally involved in tourism, giving greater priority to education or preservation. Thus, most tourism organizations do not serve only tourists, and many other organizations serve at least some tourists. The accounting is difficult. Rules, based on empirical surveys, have been developed to facilitate the calculation of satellite accounts, which permit the comparison of economic sectors at least at the national level. However, the methods have yet to be extended to smaller areas, such as local levels, where most tourism impacts are concentrated.

The result is that although huge amounts of data on tourism are available, it is extremely difficult to use the data or to access useful information, especially at the local level. Data inadequacies and the difficulty of making comparisons between tourism and other economic sectors also contribute to the frequent lack of appreciation of the significance of tourism. It is even debated whether tourism should be regarded as an industry in its own right or as a collection of activities and outputs emanating from other industries. If tourism is an industry, then it is reasonable to inquire concerning its product. The product of tourism is experiences. The characteristics of these experiences will be examined in the next section.

TOURISM EXPERIENCES

Figure 2.1 displays a simplified tourism system. It indicates that tourist-generating regions (origins) and tourist-attracting regions (destinations) are linked by transit routes. Put another way, demand, supply, and intervening distance exist. Although it is perhaps natural to focus on what occurs in the destination area, the total experience is influenced by what happens in all parts of the system. It follows that if a community interested in attracting tourism is to be successful, it must look beyond its borders, to areas of demand and means of access.

To further complicate matters, the experience of travel has temporal aspects that can be divided into five phases: anticipation, the outward journey, being on-site, the return journey, and recollection. Anticipation occurs in the place of origin, when possible destinations are considered and evaluated and plans and reservations are made. These travel components may be an important part of the tourism experience, especially with sightseers. The outward and return journey differ because they may not always involve the same routes and because they are undertaken in a different frame of mind and prominent features are viewed in reverse order. The on-site phases will be covered in greater detail in the next paragraph. The recollection phase occurs when the tourist returns home, distributes presents, and imposes holiday photographs on friends and colleagues. It may involve the wearing

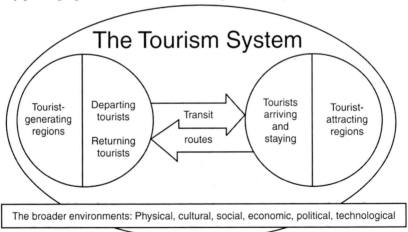

FIGURE 2.1. The tourism system.

of a named T-shirt bought at the destination, which tells others "I have been here! What about you?" The recollection phase feeds back into the decision-making process for the next trip. Of course, the process is more complex than outlined in this brief description, particularly if multiple destinations are involved.

The on-site experience is the part of the total experience that usually receives the most attention. It, too, is complex, comprising attractions, transportation, accommodations, food and beverages, quality of service, and even such seemingly mundane aspects as the quality of infrastructure, including water, electricity, and waste disposal. These services may be provided by a mix of multinational corporations and small local businesses—even, in many developing countries, through the informal sector. Thus, the tourism industry is highly fragmented, and the failure of any one component can undermine the whole experience. For example, failure occurs when the airline fails to deliver baggage until the end of a holiday, or when deficiencies in food or water quality incapacitate the consumer.

To be successful, a destination area must look beyond its borders to the origins of its clientele and the position of competitors. It must pay careful attention to the often highly fragmented operations that contribute to the visitors' experiences. Coordination and collaboration are required if the delivery of acceptable experiences is not to be left to chance. Ideally, the components of the tourism system, including the various on-site service providers, should be in balance with one another and with demand. Too much supply will lead to suboptimal use and reduced profits. Conversely, undersupply will lead to congestion, maintenance problems, and degradation of environment and experiences. Balance does not occur automatically in either the short or long term, but requires careful planning and management. In the short term, seasonality is a problem for most destination areas, and long-term growth in the number of visitors requires expanding supply. A dynamic equilibrium must be sought between the various components of supply and demand—not easy to achieve when investment requirements for a new airport, a 300-room hotel, or a waste treatment plant come in large lumps.

These observations point toward three important implications for discussions of tourism. First, tourism requires a broad perspective: it is more than just the construction and operation of hotels. Second, tourism involves both public and private sectors. Often attractions such as historic areas, parks, and beaches are under the control of the public sector, but the tourists spend their money in the private sector, on transportation, accommodations, and food. The third implication arises from the preceding one. Tourism has many of the attributes of a common property resource; the short-term interests of the private sector may encourage expansion that threatens the long-term viability of the resource on which the private sector ultimately depends. This alone is a cogent argument for careful planning and involvement of all stakeholders in the determination of the future of tourism.

TOURISM IN URBAN AREAS

Tourism is also an urbanizing force. Tourists, just as residents, require somewhere to sleep, and place demands on water, electricity, and waste assimilation capacity. In fact, they tend to be more voracious in their demands than permanent residents. In addition, the labor force required to cater to even seasonal tourists must be fed and sheltered.

Tourism occurs in settlements from the smallest hamlet to the largest city. Although tourism may be concentrated in specific areas of the city, it may blend into the cosmopolitan atmosphere found in many of the world's large urban areas. Conversely, where tourism exists in small towns, it may be highly visible as one among relatively few economic activities. Many small coastal resorts, formerly fishing communities, are now essentially unifunctional tourism destinations.

Although one might imagine tropical islands and palm-fringed beaches to be the most desirable places to visit, the reality is that major cities are the most visited tourism destinations. In Asia, this includes places such as Hong Kong, Singapore, and Bangkok. This occurs for a variety of reasons. First, transportation systems converge on major cities. Even if one is visiting a small town or more remote location, a high probability exists that the tourist will need to pass through a major city to make the necessary travel connections. Second, major cities are the location of the high-order functions, such as specialized shopping, medical and educational facilities, professional sporting events, museums, art galleries, and cultural extravaganzas, that are attractive to tourists. Major cities also possess the necessary infrastructure, such as a proliferation of high-quality accommodation facilities. Many trips are multipurpose, mixing, for example, business with pleasure. Many such trips, especially those with a business component, focus on cities, and as a result tourism in cities is often less seasonal than in other locations. Many tourists visit friends and relatives. As an increasing proportion of the population resides in urban areas, so increases the likelihood of visiting friends and relatives (VFR) trips being directed to cities. Thus, most cities have substantial tourism industries.

Analytical Techniques

If tourism is to be developed in any large or small location, it is important that the situation be assessed in a rigorous manner before critical decisions are made. Fortunately, simple analytical techniques exist that can be used to examine tourism situations. Furthermore, as the techniques are applied, they lend themselves to community participation.

For example, assessment of resources is an important task for any tourism destination. Figure 2.2 is a breadth-versus-length diagram. The horizontal axis marked *breadth* lists types of tourist attractions, in this case historical, outdoor, nightlife, and other. The offerings of the area under consideration are listed below these headings. Columns with long lists may indicate a competitive advantage in this type of provision. Conversely, where the list is short, a deficiency

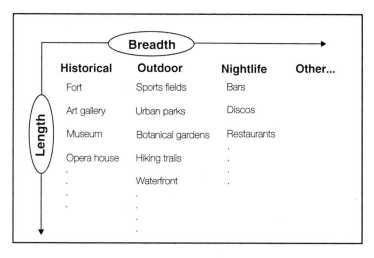

FIGURE 2.2. Breadth-versus-length diagram.

may exist. Decisions need to be made as to whether this deficiency should be made up through additional provisions, or whether these types of provision should not be made. Of course, different headings can be used for different situations, and other parts of the tourism system, such as accommodations, can be analyzed in a similar manner.

It is not enough to have a large amount of provisions of a particular type if they are not of high quality. Tourism is a highly competitive industry, and it is necessary to compare one's situation with that of competitors to see if a comparative advantage exists. Figure 2.3 is a quality-versus-variety diagram. In this diagram, for the unspecified attribute under examination, D is in the most competitive position, having both high quality and high variety. C has high quality but limited variety. Both A and B have wide variety but lower quality, with B having slightly more of the attribute than A as indicated by the larger circle.

Unless a single, isolated site is of particularly high quality, it is likely to be of less interest to tourists than places with multiple attractions. Figure 2.4 arrays morphology (monuments or other sites that one observes only from the outside, places that one can enter and explore, and complexes, which are ensembles with multiple attractions and facilities) against functional mix (monofunctional tourism, mixed, and no tourism). Such diagrams enable one to position particular places on the basis of their attributes. Such analyses are ideally the result of detailed mapping exercises, possibly facilitated by the use of geographical information systems.

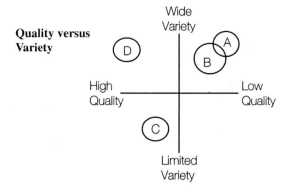

FIGURE 2.3. Quality-versus-variety diagram.

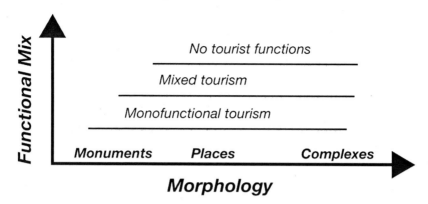

FIGURE 2.4. Morphology versus functional mix.

It will not always be possible to quantify tourism attributes of places. However, the process of undertaking such analyses in a systematic manner and, if possible, with the input of stakeholders can be beneficial to all involved. It can help to ensure that subsequent decisions are made on an informed and widely accepted body of information.

STAKEHOLDERS

Tourism development is likely to involve many stakeholders in a community, some of whom may be proponents of tourism and others who may be objectors. However, the majority of people in most communities, whether for or against, are likely to be passive (i.e., not involved). Only a minority is likely to become actively involved in promoting or resisting change. However, the players may evolve over time, and individuals may also modify their involvement over time as the issues change.

It must be recognized that the objectives of these various individuals, who are usually called stakeholders, are often quite different. Some stakeholders can be seen as the entrepreneurs responsible for identifying opportunities, investing in their development, and ensuring their successful operation. They can be from both within as well as outside the community. Conventional wisdom is that investors and entrepreneurs from within the community usually have a higher "stake" in the welfare of the residents and of the environment. However, with increasing recognition of the importance of corporate social responsibility, many outside investors now see their vested interest in ensuring a high-quality environment. Other stakeholders are those whose objective is to maintain and improve the physical and natural environment as well as the important community attributes and values. They too can be from within the community as well as from outside the community, such as the Sierra Club. In some cases they are seen as being against growth. Experience has shown that very often, well-managed and sustainable growth can meet the objectives of both the entrepreneurs as well as those concerned with the preservation of values and environment. Finally, another group of stakeholders consists of those responsible for creating culture and heritage. Community residents are often responsible for creating heritage attractions and products. In many communities, outsiders can play an important role in making this happen by bringing in new skills and knowledge. Governments at various levels play essential roles in helping to protect as well as encourage the development of various forms of heritage.

The success of any destination, as discussed in Chapter 1, relies on the ability of the various stakeholders to work effectively together in ensuring a successful sustainable destination.

WHY TOURISM?

It may appear simpleminded to ask why destination residents want tourists. The answer is seemingly obvious: the creation of jobs, incomes, and through these a higher standard of living and a more attractive community. The implications of this obvious answer, however, are far less obvious. If destination communities court tourism to improve their own standard of living, then tourism planning should be as much about planning for residents as it is about planning for tourists. Tourists are not welcomed merely so they will have a good time—although if they do, they may return and encourage others to come, since word-of-mouth is the best form of publicity. Rather, tourists are sought after for their money. In fact, destinations would be better off if tourists just sent their money and did not actually visit, since the costs of visitor management would then be circumvented. This being the case, it is curious to see tourism plans with goals and objectives specified in numbers of visitors. Such objectives are easy to achieve—just offer tourists free visits! However, the attraction of tourists is a means rather than an end. More attention should be given in tourism plans to the specification of appropriate goals and objectives and to the creation of opportunities for separating tourists from their money. The arrival of tourists is not necessarily as closely linked to expenditure as many assume. Although this may appear to be a highly mercenary position, it is one that has the interests of residents at heart, and provides tourists with a much greater freedom of choice about where to go and what to do. However, the interests of residents and tourists need not be at odds, for the best destinations are attractive places for residents and visitors alike.

HIGH STAKES

The growth of tourism has created many opportunities for new destinations to jump on the tourism bandwagon to seek their fortunes. When all else fails, it seems, try tourism. A great deal is at risk, because tourists choose to visit special, often fragile, places. Although the rewards of success are substantial, the price of failure is also high. Melaka, Malaysia, as illustrated in Figure 2.5, provides an example of what can happen when the development is not in balance with the resource.

The top two photographs show the Portuguese Fort (a) and the Dutch Church (b) and surroundings, which are a part of the colonial legacy of Melaka. The third photograph (c) shows the museum garden at the back of the house in which the treaty that gave Malaysia its independence from Britain was signed. The serenity of the garden is being compromised by the construction of an enormous hotel. The bottom row of photographs shows development totally out of scale with the historic resources and their surroundings. In the first photograph (d), new hotel construction dwarfs residential buildings. The center photograph (e) shows the development of 700 shophouses. The development includes no open space and is fronted by a cleared area on which a Sea World theme park was to be built. Access to these areas is through the historic core. Although occupancy rates were low, hotel construction continued unabated, at least until the Asian economic crisis suggested a more cautious approach.

**Melaka,
Malaysia,
Urban Tourism
Scenes**

FIGURE 2.5. Urban tourism system.

The photographs illustrate the fragility of the resources and the magnitude of changes that can be associated with tourism, and the degradation of special places and loss of amenity for both residents and visitors when adequate plans are not in place and implemented.

SUMMARY AND CONCLUSIONS

It has been argued that tourism is a major economic activity and important agent of global change, although its impacts tend to be highly concentrated in destination areas. It is a prime example of a global phenomenon with local implications. Tourism involves the provision of experiences in exchange for money. These experiences are highly complex and require input from a fragmented industry. They need to be coordinated, managed, and planned if an attractive product is to be sold to a sophisticated clientele in an increasingly competitive global marketplace. Urban areas of all sizes are major tourism destinations, and tourism is an urbanizing force. If tourism is to contribute to the well-being of residents and visitors alike, then attention should be given to both the needs of the former and the desires of the latter. Good tourism planning is as much about planning for local people as it is about planning for visitors.

REFERENCE

Mathieson, A. and Wall, G. 1982. *Tourism: Economic, Physical and Social Impacts.* London: Longman, Harlow.

Chapter 3

Community Participation
in the Royal Development Projects

Panthep Klanarongran

INTRODUCTION

Human development, particularly in the form of public participation, is integral to social development. Without support and willing participation from the public, no program or initiative conceived by government to benefit the public can wholly succeed.

His Majesty King Bhumibol Adulyadej of Thailand, with exceptional insight, has recognized this. Many of his vocational and agricultural development activities are designed to help Thai farmers become self-sufficient, and he has taken great care to make sure that local people are involved from the beginning with the projects and initiatives that will affect them. Community involvement from such an early stage ensures that the farmers have an opportunity to understand and address the problems, limitations, and potentials of each project. His Majesty regards the people of Thailand as an important resource, and his high valuation on their direct and willing participation contributes significantly to the nation's stability.

The Royal Development Study Center (RDSC), which has already implemented many projects, aims to solve problems in different contexts by encouraging a cross-pollination of ideas between technical experts, field-workers, and local people, integrating multidisciplinary approaches, coordinating among agencies, and unifying services for communities. This chapter will present some of the methods and

Community Destination Management in Developing Economies
© 2006 by The Haworth Press, Inc. All rights reserved.
doi:10.1300/5140_04

practices of community participation, whose principles for effective project implementation have been laid down by His Majesty.

ROYAL PRINCIPLES FOR SOCIAL DEVELOPMENT AND COMMUNITY PARTICIPATION

"Make it simple," is His Majesty's frequent advice. To ensure that the Royal Development Projects are understandable to local communities and appropriate to local conditions, to the ecology of the community as a whole, and to the social conditions of its members, the following concepts were developed and approved by His Majesty:

- *Voluntary involvement.* This principle states that no one is ordered to follow these initiatives. Involvement should be, instead, on a voluntary basis.
- *Self-reliance.*
- *Popular participation.*
- *Democracy.*
- *Consistency.* This principle asks that local conditions and characteristics, including topography, environment, culture, and tradition, be taken into consideration when implementing development work.
- *Community strengthening.* This principle promotes the building of a social and economic foundation that will lead to a state of sustainable self-reliance.
- *Education.* This principle encourages people to learn how to support themselves and practice agriculture using the most effective techniques available.

His Majesty has proposed the following methods to put these principles into practice:

- *Organization of groups to help solve the community's major problems.* These groups are intended to move communities toward self-reliance. Cooperatives, for example, have been organized in all the regions visited by His Majesty. Such groups facilitate the solution of community problems through joint action and thus enable the entire community to improve its economic circumstances. Many successful cooperatives have had their start in small-scale people's groups.

- *Motivation of community leaders to take the lead in development.* Through the practice of mutual support, which is characteristic of Thai society, leaders of sufficient means are encouraged to help create projects in which poorer neighbors can participate. This benefits the entire community.
- *Promotion of the development of step-by-step self-reliance.* Hasty action does not lead to success. It is important for communities first to become self-sustaining in food production. Other community development, including the growth of production for commercial purposes, can follow. His Majesty calls this "expanding from the center outward": the community should make itself strong before directing its energies and products toward the rest of the world.

A strong community receives participation and willing contributions from each individual. In project activities, members need to share their ideas in order to come up with workable solutions to the challenges they face. They must pool their resources and work cooperatively to realize their common goals. In any activity, all members must share the responsibility of work as well as the results of their efforts.

ROYAL DEVELOPMENT PROJECTS AND THEIR OBJECTIVES

His Majesty's efforts to improve the lives of Thailand's people has led to the establishment of the Royal Development Projects. The Office of the Royal Development Projects Board (RDPB) is responsible for ensuring that the royal initiatives are fully implemented. The role of the Office of RDPB is to analyze project plans, coordinate with different agencies, monitor progress, and evaluate project results.

The Royal Development Projects have three main objectives. The first is to address immediate community problems. The second is to disseminate information, knowledge, and advanced technology that is adapted to suit local wisdom and ways of life. The third objective is to help individuals, particularly the less fortunate, improve their own well-being and provide themselves with enough to eat and live comfortably.

THE ROYAL DEVELOPMENT STUDY CENTERS

The Royal Development Study Center was established to address challenges distinct to the conditions of each area, with the relevant government department serving as the main coordinating agency. The primary goal of the royal initiative is community involvement. Six centers exist, available in all regions of the country: Khao Hin Sorn RDSC, located in Chachoengsao Province; Huai Sai RDSC, located in Phetchaburi Province; Kung Krabaen Bay RDSC, located in Chanthaburi Province; Puparn RDSC, located in Sakon Nakhon Province; Huai Hong Khrai RDSC, located in Chiang Mai Province; and Pikun Thong RDSC, located in Narathiwat Province.

Despite varying objectives and emphasis, the tasks of all six RDSCs are similar:

1. To conduct study and research toward the creation of guidelines and approaches to development appropriate to the different conditions of each area or region. Care will be taken that these methods benefit not only those in the region itself, but in surrounding areas as well.
2. To serve as a clearinghouse for the exchange of knowledge and experience among academics, development workers, and the community at large. Conclusions should address, and be applicable to, real-world situations.
3. To serve as a center for integrated development patterns and be a model for multidisciplinary concepts that can produce large, tangible benefits for specific areas.
4. To build and reinforce close coordination in project planning, implementation, and management among different government agencies within an intersectoral framework.
5. To function as a center for the dissemination of research, experimentation, and demonstration of operational success in all relevant agricultural fields—in other words, to be a living natural museum for agriculture.

Once the center, working together with various officials, has consolidated this knowledge, the next task is to spread that knowledge to the public and encourage community participation.

EXAMPLES OF COMMUNITY PARTICIPATION

Huai Sai Royal Development Study Center

In the past, Thailand was rich in natural resources and wildlife. In a little over 65 years, those natural resources have been almost completely depleted as a result of inefficient farming techniques and public encroachment onto previously pristine land. Immediate action was commissioned by His Majesty to restore the destroyed zones. The work emphasized rehabilitation of deteriorated forests by reforestation in a way that crop cultivation could be carried out at the same time. Water resources were provided to support these activities.

However, these efforts would not have been successful without cooperation from all parties, especially those whose interests were directly affected. The center also encouraged local people within the project area to live and work in a sustainable and environmentally friendly way. The community was encouraged to care for while also making use of the forest resources and crops. Once cooperation had been established, the community no longer needed to encroach on the forests for sustenance.

Methods for Encouraging Public Involvement

On visits to each destination, His Majesty explains the essentials of the project and the ways in which it will benefit the community. If the community agrees to the project, the next step can be taken. This step involves the organization of training courses at the RDSC and the simultaneous dispatch of officials to provide assistance and advice. It is an opportunity for everyone to contribute to problem solving through an exchange of ideas.

After the Huai Sai RDSC carried out extensive promotion and training on cultivation of chemical-free vegetables, farmers, now better equipped to plan their own production of fresh produce for market, came together under the name "Farmers' Unifying Force Group." This joint effort brought together farmers, businessmen, and government officials to share information and opinions on their experiences with agricultural business and the marketing of chemical-free vegetables. At first the group consisted of only nine or ten members, and several factors made production very difficult: the lack of knowledge and skills, poor soil conditions, pests, and dependence on a single market. But with members' unified resolve and steady determination, along with keen support from the Huai Sai RDSC. Based on statistics from 2001, the Farmers' Unifying Force Group has 22 members. On average, each member earns 3,000 to 4,500 baht per month (70 to 100 U.S. dollars). The group has also accumulated a central savings fund of 27,140 baht (700 U.S. dollars), to be spent as needed and distributed as dividends.

The Wat Mongkol Chaipattana Area Development Project

Wat Mongkol Chaipattana in Saraburi Province is regarded as a model for the "new theory" practice. It focuses on the development of both natural and human resources by applying the principles of *bor-wor-ror*, which consists of *baan* (home or community), *wat* (temple), and *ratchakarn* (government). His Majesty recognizes that the temple can play an important role in influencing the practice of rural development today.

The temple is a center of spiritual unity, and can contribute to the balance of the development of both mind and material achievement. The temple is also a center for community coordination and cooperation, and can be a place for the acquisition of knowledge, training, and the exchange of agricultural technology. The "new theory," the purpose of which is to provide all members of the community with better, self-sustaining ways of living, demonstrates that farmers who own even a small piece of land can increase their farm production to a level sufficient for a certain measure of self-sustenance through proper management of soil and water resources.

Three stages are included in the implementation of the new theory:

1. Farmers look to their families to contribute labor, and receive necessary technical assistance from government officials. For effective management of soil and water, a piece of land is divided into four parts, using a basic ratio of 30:30:30:10, which is then adjusted to suit the conditions of each area. Thirty percent of the land is set aside for use as a pond, for the raising of fish and the provision of water for crop irrigation and household consumption. Another 30 percent of the land is dedicated to the cultivation of rice, the staple food in the Thai diet; from this rice

crop, the whole family can have enough to eat year-round. Another 30 percent of the land is planted with perennial trees, field crops, fruit crops, vegetables, etc. These are used to supply daily meals, and the surplus is sold to earn extra income. The remaining land, 10 percent, is used for residential areas, infrastructure, farm facilities, animal housing, and other needs.

2. Once the first stage has been successfully implemented, farmers are urged to join forces in groups or cooperatives to help create or maintain effective production and marketing of their produce. The second stage directly concerns community participation and relies on group unity to gain bargaining power against merchants who could otherwise suppress prices. The farmers are then able to sell or even buy agricultural produce at reasonable prices, which in turn allows them to cut expenses.

3. The third stage also requires community participation. Once farmers successfully pass the second stage, they can make contacts with sources of funding such as banks or companies for help with investment and improvement of quality of life.

The Mangrove Rehabilitation and Development Project

Within this project are two subprojects: the Yaring Mangrove Education Center in Pattani Province and the Hua Khao Community-Led Mangrove Rehabilitation in Songkhla Province. This project's success depends again on community participation. The Hua Khao fishing community in Songkhla Province was once enriched by mangrove habitats. However, in the past 20 to 30 years, increased population, growing infrastructure, port construction, and other factors have led to the deterioration of the mangrove forests. In addition, the community itself is now facing many social challenges.

His Majesty proposed the restoration of the health of the mangrove forests and other natural resources. He suggested that community participation along with technical approaches be a main element of this project since local community participation is vital to natural resource management. Accordingly, the project involves both a program of intervention and a process of empowering the community to undertake its own development and manage its own resources. Local people now play a crucial role in the plantation, maintenance, and utilization of its output.

The strategies of the Community-Led Mangrove Rehabilitation project include the following:

- The local community itself is a main actor for mangrove rehabilitation.
- Preparation must be based on an understanding of communal data analysis.
- The local community and its leaders are provided with the knowledge and skills they need to rehabilitate the mangrove forest.
- The community works with all concerned parties, enhancing its future management potential.

Through community efforts, the mangrove replanting program has resulted in 50 hectares of new mangrove forest, which have generated many positive social and environmental results. The planting undertaken by villagers shows excellent growth. The mangrove rehabilitation group was eventually formed in 1995, to take a leading role in the project activities.

EDUCATION-ORIENTED TOURISM

In addition to the locally and regionally focused functions previously described, The RDSC will also be promoted as one of the country's education-oriented tourism destinations. The ultimate goal of the center's activities is to enhance, through education, all aspects of the rural Thai standard of living while conserving natural resources and the whole environment; therefore, the center is concerned not just with tourism, but particularly with education-oriented tourism.

For example, the Huai Sai RDSC in Phetchaburi Province has beautiful beaches, forests, and national parks as well as a rich ancient heritage. Preliminary studies have been launched and serious consideration has been given to exploring the possible promotion of the center as an educational tourist destination.

The center's four goals for tourism are as follows:

1. The establishment of an information center at the Huai Sai RDSC headquarters, including such components as indoor and outdoor exhibitions and publicity materials such as tourist guidebooks,

informative tapes in different languages, and a shop selling souvenirs and local agricultural produce.

2. The education and preparation of staff to render high-standard services to tourists, involving the arrangement of training courses for locals to qualify as tour guides and other tourism-related jobs.

3. The development of activities along the tour, including, for example, botanic or herbal gardens and mangrove forests, a zoo, cattle raising, chemical-free vegetable cultivation, and demonstrations of household industries such as gemstone cutting. Accommodations would also be available in the forms of camping tents and homestays to give visitors a chance to observe the villagers' way of life. The educational experience would be augmented with recreational activities such as sailing, canoeing, bicycle riding, and horseback riding.

4. The provision of clearly defined management guidelines and roles for all involved parties, particularly within the community, to encourage active participation. This task includes:

   a. the assignment of management roles for all activities and the formation of groups responsible for the operation of each activity;

   b. the provision of advice and support for these groups and the construction of basic infrastructure;

   c. The securing of support from the private sector or other nongovernmental organizations to provide funds and assist in coordination at the local level; and

   d. the establishment of shareholding, seventy percent by local people and thirty percent by the Chaipattana Foundation, which serves as the main coordinator and financial supporter for Royal Development Projects, particularly in the initial stage.

CONCLUSION

In accordance with His Majesty's principles of development, the Royal Development Projects are often given a variety of objectives. These projects were founded to encourage economic development and a higher income level for Thai farmers as well as to promote social development, build community security and strength, and improve the overall quality of life. They also hope to promote the preservation of the Thai culture and way of life.

One of the Royal Development Project's most important principles is that individuals within the community must participate in decision-making from the start of each project. Communities must choose their own direction of development and become receptive to future external development trends. To this end, His Majesty presents the project and the expected results to the community, then asks if they are willing to try the project. If they are willing, he requests that those who will be benefiting and those who will be making sacrifices come to an agreement among themselves. When a unanimous accord is reached, local leaders, from village and community heads to district officers and provincial governors, are summoned to acknowledge the agreement. They are also asked to take such initial steps as the settlement of problems of land ownership. Then His Majesty brings in the agencies concerned to manage the administrative and technical sides of project operation until the project is completed.

His Majesty's thinking ranges widely in diverse areas of the development process, and throughout the past half century he has greatly improved the lives of the Thai people. It is a privilege to present His Majesty's initiatives as a good and practical example of the crucial role of community participation in social development.

Chapter 4

Community Planning
for Tourism Development:
Klong Khwang Case Study,
Nakhon Ratchasima
Province, Thailand

Pawinee Sunalai

INTRODUCTION

With growing international interest in community-based tourism, the maintenance of cultural and environmental integrity in small, fragile communities has never been more critical. This integrity may easily be lost through shortsighted, harmful development schemes whose goal is quick economic gain rather than sustainable community development. In this scenario, both tourists and communities ultimately lose. The tourism development of small communities needs to be actively planned, developed, and managed, with a strong emphasis on community involvement and sustainable development principles. The Thai village of Klong Khwang is one such example.

Located in the Nakhon Ratchasima Province (Korat) in the northeast region of Thailand, Klong Khwang is 30 minutes by automobile west of Korat, the province's capital city. The village belongs to Tambon (subdistrict) Sema, which includes 13 villages, and the Amphoe (district) Sung Noen, with a total population of 75,000. The village of Klong Khwang contains slightly more than one hundred households.

Community Destination Management in Developing Economies
© 2006 by The Haworth Press, Inc. All rights reserved.
doi:10.1300/5140_05

It has three main attractions: a reclining Buddha (see Photo 4.1), the stone wheel of Wat Thammachak Semaram (see Photo 4.2), and an archaeological site (see Photo 4.3).

As a tourism destination, Klong Khwang is still in a formative stage. However, as development progresses, efforts are being made to

PHOTO 4.1. Reclining Buddha.

PHOTO 4.2. The stone wheel of Wat Thammachak Semaram.

PHOTO 4.3. Archaeological site of ancient city in Sema.

help the community identify and achieve its tourism objectives through the emphasis of principles that support community participation, environmental sustainability, and cultural integrity.

This chapter will discuss the process of tourism planning in the Klong Khwang community, carried out with the assistance of the Canadian Universities Consortium Urban Environmental Management (CUC UEM) project through the Training and Technology Transfer Program (TTTP) at the Asian Institute of Technology (AIT).

THE TOURISM PLANNING PROCESS OF KLONG KHWANG

The community of Klong Khwang requested technical assistance on tourism and planning management from the TTTP team. The village presently hosts small groups of local tourists who mainly come to pay their respects to the Reclining Buddha and the stone wheel of Wat Thammachak Semaram, and to visit the archaeological site. Visitors typically spend upwards of one hour visiting Klong Khwang and contribute a total of approximately 10,000 baht per month (240 U.S. dollars) through *wat* (temple) donations.

The goal of the planning process was to develop the community in a sustainable and inclusive way. Key participants involved in the planning process included the village headman, a women's group, public health volunteers, a village committee, the subdistrict administration organization, and a youth representative. The first task in the planning process was to define the development goals and objectives that would guide the direction of tourism development in Klong Khwang. The community's stated aim was to generate additional income from tourism, using public consultation and a mock tourism day to encourage community involvement in the tourism planning process.

Public Consultation

Several informal meetings were organized with key actors, particularly the Klong Khwang headman, the village committee, and the women's group, to further define the reasons for the community's desire to develop tourism and to discuss the types of benefits and the numbers of tourists they expected. Development controls as well as issues of interpretation, promotion, and marketing were identified, and the future impacts of such tourism on villagers, including possible effects on cultural life, were also discussed. TTTP members encouraged the key participants to define tourism products and the direction of tourism development for their village, with a high priority placed on environmental and cultural preservation.

Other villagers received these messages through meetings called by the village headman and community members at which diverse views and interests were well received. Klong Khwang's headman, who is very enthusiastic about tourism, was instrumental in bringing about this crucial step. The headman described the advantages and disadvantages of tourism and proposed activities to the community in accordance with the tourism plan that the TTTP team had assisted in developing. Among these activities were the creation of an information center and parking lot, the development of agricultural products and souvenirs, the establishment of a savings group, and work on agricultural products, according to the King of Thailand's project principles (discussed in Chapter 3).

Mock Tourism Day

Effective community participation is an essential principle of sustainable development, but it is also often one of the most difficult to put into practice. Responding to this challenge, the Klong Khwang villagers, with help from the TTTP team, conducted a full-scale "mock tourism day" in order to build the community's readiness to embrace tourism. The tourism day had several objectives. It was designed to provide villagers with an opportunity to witness a significant flow of visitors into their community and thus experience tourists and tourism-resident issues. It also provided an opportunity to test the capacity of the community's infrastructure and to evaluate the site's attractiveness as a tourism destination. Finally, it enabled residents to make an informed decision about whether to accept and develop tourism as a village activity over a longer period of time.

In the mock-tourism exercise, a team of students, friends, and family from the TTTP posed as "tourists for a day" in Klong Khwang. More than forty visitors took part. The distribution of men and women was equal, ranging in age from the midteens to the early fifties (see Photo 4.4). The overall program as well as specific tourism activities were developed by the village headman and other community members. The community was very well organized, providing English-speaking tour guides, planning an interesting sightseeing itinerary, and offering a large buffet lunch. Visitor evaluations confirmed that the "tourists" had had an enjoyable and educational day. More important, the community experienced the demands and opportunities associated with hosting a large group of tourists.

PHOTO 4.4. Mock tour.

This tourism day proved to be a good foundation for experience-based community discussion of basic tourism issues, such as the desirability of large tour groups, the timing of visits, the distribution of economic benefits, the influence on daily community life, and the adequacy of present facilities and infrastructure—including waste management and toilet facilities.

TTTP members facilitated the planning process in the following ways:

- They prepared visual representations of strategic community sites as a guide for the physical development of the village to encourage community participation.
- They designed marketing and promotional materials, including brochures and postcards, delegating responsibility to local officials for supplying data, such as key points of interest in Klong Khwang and text for print materials (see Figure 4.1).
- They developed and described various components of the development plan.

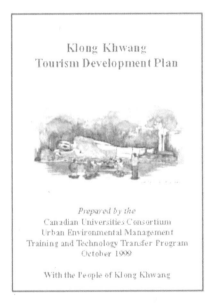

FIGURE 4.1. Plan and brochures.

THE TOURISM PLAN

Previously, Klong Khwang's economy was based almost entirely on agriculture, with rice as the main crop. However, tourism has been identified as a potential force for economic development, and the community is already experiencing economic benefits from visitors, who come primarily to see the Reclining Buddha.

Through the planning process, the TTTP assisted Klong Khwang in the development of a community tourism plan and proposed three possible scenarios: minimal, moderate, and large-scale tourism development. The community chose to proceed with a model for tourism development that would initially produce modest numbers of visitors. This level of development positions tourism as a seasonal activity separate from, and for the most part not disruptive to, the existing agricultural base of the community. Villagers believed this would be the least intrusive way to provide much-needed income at specific times of the year.

These modest goals require a much lower level of involvement on the part of residents, and also a smaller financial investment than for a more ambitious and far-reaching plan. Limited tourism development and concrete economic goals also recognize the fragility of the community: its limited carrying capacity, restricted budgets, and its desire to protect the community's agricultural base. This is not to say that tourism is not important to Klong Khwang but rather that it is one component of the community's overall development objectives.

The headman of Klong Khwang village, who has a broad vision of development of Klong Khwang, says that "a plan is a bridge to the future." In order to strengthen community involvement in ongoing development projects, Klong Khwang has set up a village committee as an advisory board for development activities. This board includes a monk, a teacher, volunteers, and someone appointed to look after the interests of the monastery. One year after receiving assistance from the TTTP, the village of Klong Khwang began implementing its plan for tourism development step by step.

Community Cooperative

In accordance with to a model of moderate tourism development, Klong Khwang established an occupational cooperative with a small investment of 9,400 baht (229 U.S. dollars). The cooperative comprises five working groups: production, marketing, finance, auditing, and sales. Each group selects its head, and the village headman acts as a chairman of the cooperative. Its objectives include the following:

- To generate additional income from tourism for the benefit of the village.
- To increase the number of employed people.
- To promote local goods made from agricultural products, such as banana chips, banana candy, shampoo, incense sticks, and artificial flowers, and to promote Klong Khwang village in general.

This cooperative had 60 members when last evaluated in 2003. To encourage members to contribute their time, members have agreed that anyone who works regularly receives a 75 percent dividend every month, whereas those who are not working receive 10 percent each year. Fifteen percent of the profit goes to the savings cooperative, which deposits this money in the bank to provide loans and emergency assistance to cooperative members. Before purchasing anything from outside the community, the cooperative tries to use raw materials found in the village (see Photo 4.5).

PHOTO 4.5. Community cooperative.

Product Development

Self-sufficiency for communities is the objective, but the provision of outside assistance toward that goal is crucial. Provincial government agencies have encouraged local people to generate supplementary income in their leisure time by training the community in the development of agricultural products. Total profit generated from selling local products such as banana chips and candy, shampoo, incense sticks and artificial flowers is around 12,000 baht per month (292 U.S. dollars).

Other souvenirs offered by Klong Khwang village include framed pictures of Klong Khwang attractions, key chains, and miniature Buddhas in souvenir booths similar to the one shown in Photo 4.6. These souvenirs can generate income of around 10,000 baht per month (243 U.S. dollars). However, due to lack of skilled human resources—but not lack of ability—the villagers hire a nonvillager to do the work rather than producing the souvenirs themselves. The headman is now trying to encourage and train unemployed villagers to do this work.

Facilities, Services, and Infrastructure

The government upgraded road connections to Klong Khwang village. Public telephones and washrooms have been provided for

PHOTO 4.6. Souvenir booth.

tourists. Sufficient signage in both Thai and English is in place from the main road into the village itself. No homestay or guesthouse is being developed since the community has chosen not to provide this amenity.

Income Distribution

The final distribution of the income generated by tourism in Klong Khwang is an important issue. Klong Khwang has three sources of income from visitors: donations, the sale of agricultural products, and the sale of souvenirs. Klong Khwang provides free flowers and incense for visitors to pay their respects to the Buddha. This practice is a tradition of Klong Khwang. In many other places in Thailand these offerings would not be given away, but sold. Money from donations is being spent on improvements and maintenance for the temple, and also for the toilets provided for tourists.

Profit from agricultural products is distributed to the members of the cooperative as described earlier. Net profits from the sale of souvenirs are distributed among the villagers who sell the goods and the cooperative itself.

Monitoring the Impacts of Tourism

The impact of tourism on the Klong Khwang community is roughly monitored through the observations of the village headman, interviews with villagers, and the analysis of statistics. In general, the overview of tourism development in Klong Khwang is good in terms of economic development as well as environmental and cultural conservation.

Since the start of the planning process, the number of tourists has increased from 1,100 to 3,000 visitors per month, with commensurate increases of income for the village. Currently, no solid waste management system is in place for Klong Khwang. The community usually burns or buries waste. Solid waste has not yet posed a problem to the community, although the number of visitors in Klong Khwang is increasing. The headman provides information on waste separation, and offers suggestions on what to sell, burn, or bury. The Subdistrict Administration Organization plans to establish a solid waste system for the Sema subdistrict.

Every house in the village has its own wastewater catchment, from which wastewater is eventually reabsorbed underground. Tourists normally spend only a few hours in the village, so they do not yet pose a wastewater disposal problem. However, underground water pollution could be an issue in the near future if plans are not made to accommodate the increasing numbers of visitors.

The village headman feels that the attitude of the community has changed positively toward tourism. The community is friendlier than in the past, and has become used to providing necessary information to tourists. Even modes of dress have become more attractive to tourists, since the headman has encouraged the villagers to wear traditional Thai clothes. Better relationships have developed among the villagers themselves.

MANAGEMENT CHALLENGES

One of the continuing challenges facing Klong Khwang is the dearth of marketing skill. The market for local products is still very small, and improved packaging is required. The governmental agencies responsible for these areas—such as the regional Tourism Authority of Thailand or the provincial government—should support Klong Khwang, and include it as one of the destinations on the Korat tourism circuit.

CONCLUSION

As Klong Khwang has become increasingly recognized as a model of positive rural tourism development, the headman has been invited by various agencies and organizations to discuss the ways the village has been able to involve the community in its development projects. Klong Khwang has also been recognized by the Asia-Pacific Economic Cooperation (APEC) as one of good examples of community-based tourism in the Asia-Pacific region.

As Klong Khwang has developed its tourism industry, a number of important lessons have been learned about the best ways to promote caution and economy among villagers, protect against failure, and ensure resources for long-term benefits.

- The village headperson is an important factor for community-based tourism in Thailand. Without active support from and the collaboration of the headperson it is very difficult to encourage people to participate effectively in tourism planning and management.
- The community planning process used in Klong Khwang can be replicated in other communities. This success depends very much on the headperson's vision, the respect villagers accord the headperson, and the equitability with which the benefits of tourism are distributed in the community.
- A cooperative is a good way to make sure that these benefits are distributed equitably. A 75 percent dividend to working members of the cooperative provides a good incentive to participate in village activities.
- Buddhism is integral to the Thai culture and lifestyle. A community with a temple or Buddha as its tourist attraction will need to understand how to balance tourism development with religious and cultural preservation.
- Donations from tourists at Klong Khwang are spent on maintenance and improvement of the temple—a significant characteristic of Klong Khwang village that has not changed because of the development.

Chapter 5

Cumulative Impact Assessment of Hotel Development in Siem Reap, Cambodia

William A. Ross

INTRODUCTION

Because of its proximity to Angkor Wat, a United Nations Education, Scientific and Cultural Organization (UNESCO) World Heritage Site, Siem Reap Town receives more visitors than anywhere else in Cambodia. As a result, many new hotels have been planned or are under construction. In collaboration with the Royal Cambodian Government, the Canadian Universities Consortium undertook a preliminary environmental impact assessment of this hotel expansion.

The assessment focused on four important impacts that the expansion might have upon the town: solid waste management, water and sewage management, energy use and air quality, and socioeconomic effects. The cumulative effects of these new hotels, along with many other past, present, and future human activities in Siem Reap Town, were potentially significant, and recommendations were made for each of these possible impacts.

The most important indicators, identified by people living in and near Siem Reap Town, were those with the potential to adversely affect

This chapter was developed based on research carried out under the leadership of the author with the assistance of Jason Husack, Glenda Koh, Hans Luu, and Kelly Skeith, graduate students in the Faculty of Environmental Design, University of Calgary.

human health and well-being and also, perhaps especially, those that could limit the potential of tourism to make life for Cambodians better. While selecting effective ways to mitigate these effects, emphasis was placed on cost-effective measures that could be easily implemented by hotel operators, could make for more sustainable tourism developments, and could be funded with international development aid.

PRELIMINARY ENVIRONMENTAL IMPACT ASSESSMENT OF HOTEL DEVELOPMENT

Overview

This Preliminary Environmental Impact Assessment Report of Hotel Development in Siem Reap, Cambodia, is the major component of the Canadian Universities Consortium project, carried out in cooperation with the Ministry of Environment of the Royal Government of Cambodia. The Canadian Universities Consortium and the Cambodian Ministry of Environment together agreed that the Canadian Universities Consortium would undertake an environmental impact assessment (EIA) of hotel development in the area. This project was funded by the Canadian International Development Agency.

This preliminary report identifies the most important environmental and social effects of hotel development and provides management recommendations for hotel owners and decision makers. The report serves as a basis for both management and the ongoing study of the effects of hotel development in Siem Reap.

The main function of this component of the project was to initiate the EIA process by carrying out the following main activities:

- Communicating with hotel and guesthouse owners, managers, and government officials about the EIA project
- Gathering relevant information
- Analyzing information
- Making recommendations based on that analysis

Background

Siem Reap Town is located seven kilometers from the major tourist attraction in Cambodia, the World Heritage Site of Angkor Wat. The region is presently undergoing rapid growth and expansion as a direct result of this tourism. Both local companies and international hotel developers have responded to the increase of international and Cambodian tourists in the region with investment and new development. The Royal Cambodian Government's initiation of this EIA of hotel development acknowledges that the cumulative environmental and social impacts of tourism must be addressed as part of a sound economic development strategy (for a full discussion of cumulative effects and their assessment, see Ross, 1998).

Methodology

This EIA report was prepared over a ten-week period, which included a two-week site visit to Siem Reap. During this visit, the research team conducted interviews and collected primary and secondary data. The visit coincided with a three-day EIA workshop for Cambodian government employees and other selected individuals. The remainder of the study period was spent in Thailand at the Asian Institute of Technology, assembling other information used to prepare the full report (Skeith et al., 2000), an analysis of the observations, interviews, and data gathered during the site visit. Very little quantitative data was employed in this analysis.

Content of the Full Report

The full report, from which this article has been extracted, covers four main areas:

1. Description of the current physical, regulatory, and social environment
2. Assessment of the impacts of hotel development
3. Recommendations for mitigating those impacts
4. Recommendations for the continuation of the EIA process

This shortened article is similar in structure, but provides significantly less detail.

Major Findings

The research team surveyed hotel activities to create a list of present and future social and environmental impacts. The present impacts were included as an indication of future impacts, and also as an indication of cumulative impacts, which proved to be an important component of the assessment. While compiling the list, the project assumed that hotel development would proceed in its current manner and at its present rate for the foreseeable future. Six criteria, developed in consultation with people from Siem Reap Province, were applied to the list of impacts to narrow the report's focus. Participants included local (provincial) Department of the Environment representatives, Ministry of the Environment representatives from the national capital, local commune chiefs, local police, tourism regulators, and hotel operators. The research team in Siem Reap interviewed others, mainly hotel and guesthouse operators and tourism officials. The issues were considered in terms of the following six criteria:

1. Seriousness of impacts
2. Ubiquity of activity
3. Importance to the community and decision makers
4. Economic development
5. Aesthetics
6. Human health (Skeith et al., 2000, pp. 30-33)

Using these criteria, the impacts were narrowed to the following four areas of focus:

1. *Water and sewage management.* Water management refers to the reliable supply of clean drinking water. Sewage management refers to the disposal of dirty water and human waste (see Table 5.1).
2. *Solid waste management.* Solid waste refers to all waste produced by a hotel—from initial construction, through operation and maintenance, to demolition (see Table 5.2).
3. *Socioeconomic impacts.* Hotel development necessarily affects the human population. The full report addresses some of the social, cultural, and economic impacts of tourism in general, and of hotel development specifically (see Table 5.3).
4. *Energy consumption and air quality.* Energy efficiency is determined by investigating the impacts of energy consumption on the environment and recommending measures to reduce energy use and thus reduce any undesirable effects (see Table 5.4).

TABLE 5.1. Mitigation measures for water and sewage management.

Type	Hotel-Level Measures	Government-Level Measures
Direct intervention measures	• Investigate water treatment processes • Pretreat sewage before discharging • Use treated sewage sludge in alternative ways • Investigate waste stabilization ponds • Investigate use of natural or constructed wetlands for long-term treatment of sewage sludge	• Regulate flow rate of Siem Reap River • Subsidize hotels' mitigation measures • Implement infrastructure development projects
Policy measures	• Perform a water audit • Develop monitoring programs to collect data on water and sewage and to evaluate effectiveness of mitigation measures regularly • Develop water conservation plans for bathrooms and laundry services • Monitor and regulate water pressure throughout building • Adopt "green purchasing" guidelines for all business purchases	• Strengthen regulations concerning environmental and sanitation standards for hotels and businesses • Incorporate international standards into regulatory framework • Improve compliance monitoring and enforcement of regulations • Institute economic instruments for the regulation of sewage management • Draft a sewage management subdecree • Set timelines for implementing mitigation measures and reaching environmental performance objectives
Education and training measures	• Create visible, participatory systems • Provide training to staff • Attempt to change visitor attitudes	• Use workshops and seminars to raise awareness and disseminate information • Publish educational information on water and sewage management for hotels, business, and the public • Develop voluntary guidelines that specify a minimum level of energy conservation in all business sectors

TABLE 5.2. Mitigation measures for solid waste.

Type	Hotel-Level Measures	Government-Level Measures
Direct intervention measures	• Use good design to allow for future expansion with a minimum of renovations; be flexible for future needs • Use durable materials • Practice "green pur-chasing" • Implement purchasing guidelines • Compost • Use anaerobic digestion: on-site, cooperatively, or on a community-wide scale • Work with community to establish market for recyclables	• Regulate dumping sites • Create proper landfill sites • Implement or subsidize biodegradation or composting programs • Expand market for biodegradation byproducts • Levy surcharges on nonrecyclables • Levy refundable deposits on recyclables • Establish recycling program • Encourage markets for recyclables
Policy measures	• Encourage hotels to develop individual solid waste management policies	• Require waste management policies for hotels • Enact "polluter pays" legislation in conjunction with solid waste subdecree
Education and training measures	• Create visible, participatory systems • Provide training to staff • Attempt to change visitor attitudes	• Publish "green" guidelines for hotels • Establish demonstration projects

Recommendations

In each of these four focus areas, recommendations were made to help minimize the environmental and social effects of hotel development. Implementation of these recommendations can enable tourism and hotel development in Siem Reap to become more culturally, environmentally, and economically sustainable.

These recommendations, summarized in the following tables, are divided into those to be undertaken by hotels and those to be under-

TABLE 5.3. Socioeconomic mitigation measures.

Type	Hotel-Level Measures	Government-Level Measures
Direct intervention measures	• Communicate with staff and community regarding hotel operations • Create changes sensitive to staff and community needs	• Consult public with regard to development issues • Create projects to address cultural heritage
Policy measures	• Create flexible policies and management practices such as profit sharing, partnerships with the community, job sharing, and equal opportunity for local residents	• Imitate community development activities that build social and economic strength • Encourage community-based economic activities • Standardize labor practices • Establish design guidelines
Education and training measures	• Provide adequate training to staff to mitigate socioeconomic impacts	• Encourage education and training in the areas of management, health and safety, and heritage preservation

taken by the government and by other organizations. The recommendations were chosen not only with respect to their effectiveness but also with respect to the situation in Cambodia. Thus, in a poor country such as Cambodia the availability of international aid would be important for infrastructure upgrades, such as a sewage treatment facility or a water distribution system.

On the other hand, no permanent environmental improvement is likely to happen without the commitment of those most directly involved, in this case hotel operators. In suggesting hotel measures, the measures focused on were those that were most likely to benefit hotels financially in addition to contributing to better environmental management. Thus "no regrets" measures—measures that save energy and are cost-effective—were identified and recommended. More important, measures that made hotels more attractive to international

TABLE 5.4. Mitigation measures for energy use.

Type	Hotel-Level Measures	Government-Level Measures
Direct intervention measures	• Continue with existing energy conservation measures and evaluate these measures regularly to identify areas for improvement • Improve existing fuel storage practices by using high-quality storage tanks, installing secondary containment devices, and developing procedures for maintenance and the handling of spills/leaks • Introduce energy-efficient lighting fixtures and consider energy-saving appliances for future purchases • Use existing appliances more efficiently	• Subsidize energy audits of individual businesses or business sectors • Offer financial incentives for energy conservation • Subsidize equipment replacement or facility renovation • Upgrade and expand public power supply
Policy measures	• Future hotel development should incorporate energy efficiency into building design • Perform an energy audit to learn more about present usage patterns and identify areas for improved energy management	• Develop fuel tank and fuel storage regulations • Regulate use of CFCs • Specify minimum energy conservation requirements for new hotels and businesses being planned • Set target objectives and timelines for action for businesses and hotels
Education and training measures	• Create visible, participatory systems • Provide training to staff • Attempt to change visitor attitudes	• Develop sector-specific energy conservation education • Develop voluntary guidelines specifying a minimum level of energy conservation in all business sectors • Seek international development aid to assist in environmental management demonstration projects • Consult with local communities and businesses to obtain their participation in the implementation of environmental management initiatives

clients desiring environmentally sensitive accommodations were also recommended.

Tables 5.1 through 5.4 describe our recommendations for the four focus areas. For more detail, refer to the full report (Skeith et al., 2000). The recommendations have been grouped into the following three methods of intervention:

1. *Direct intervention.* These measures are practical, usually phys- ical actions that can be taken to mitigate impacts.
2. *Policy-level intervention.* This term refers to the creation of change using such tools as regulations, standards, and laws.
3. *Education and training measures.* These measures recognize that changes in attitude toward management, tourism, and ev- eryday life are integral to the mitigation of environmental impacts. These recommendations consist of programs and ideas to provide further education and expertise on environmental issues.

When the study was carried out in 1999, it was feared that in the absence of effective environmental management the tourism boom in Siem Reap Province could be short-lived. This conclusion was based on the experience of other destinations where poor environmental im- pacts are seen as unacceptable to international tourists. However, vis- itor numbers continue to grow in Siem Reap despite field observa- tions in 2005 that showed that few environmental measures have been instituted. Interviews with key officials indicate that environmental management is still urgently needed. Given the enormous attraction of Angkor Wat, tour operators and tourist tend to be more willing to overlook the poor environmental conditions. However, an outbreak of disease brought about by these conditions would seriously affect the success of the destination.

CONCLUSION

In addition to the work described, the research team suggested that involvement from the inhabitants of Siem Reap would help to obtain a better picture of the impacts of hotel development and of possible means of mitigating them.

This EIA work has identified a number of ways to avoid environmental problems, relying primarily on cost-effective means and those that should attract international development-aid funding. One very important message is that it is important to deal with the cumulative impacts of all human activity, past, present, and future, and not just with the effects of the hotels alone.

REFERENCES

Ross, W.A. 1998. Cumulative effects assessment: Learning from Canadian case studies. *Impact Assessment and Project Appraisal* 16 (4): 267-276.

Skeith, K., G. Koh, J. Husack, H. Luu, W. Ross, and W. Jamieson. 2000. *Environmental Impact Assessment of Hotel Development in Siem Reap Town, Cambodia.* Bangkok, Thailand: Asian Institute of Technology.

Chapter 6

Interpretation and Tourism

Walter Jamieson

INTRODUCTION

The more connected and engaged visitors feel with a community—that is, the more memorable their experiences are, and the more unique, accessible, and authentic they feel the community and its people to be—the longer they are likely to stay, and the more likely they are to return. Longer stays and repeat visits can generate considerable economic benefits for the community. When these visitors return home, they are also more likely to tell friends about their experiences. Word-of-mouth is a very effective promotion strategy. Interpretation is a powerful way to create this type of visitor engagement.

In the same way that translators interpret across languages, communities can interpret their heritage so that it is meaningful across different cultures. Interpretation—explaining a community's story in an engaging, vibrant way—is a useful tool for tourism destination management and conservation. It can be used to encourage respect and appropriate behavior from tourists and can also promote feelings of pride and awareness within a community.

Every community has stories about its history, people, and cultural heritage. Developing a program of interpretation puts a community in control of how these stories are presented to others. An interpretive program also encourages tourists to value and appreciate local heritage in the same way that community residents do. That bond can lead to a successful, healthy, and sustainable tourism industry.

Community Destination Management in Developing Economies
© 2006 by The Haworth Press, Inc. All rights reserved.
doi:10.1300/5140_07

Interpretation not only makes tourists' visits richer but it also gives communities a tool to manage and control tourism and tourists in their area. By interpreting a community and providing reasons behind (for example) clothing restrictions, tourists will be less likely to offend residents and more likely to adhere to local customs. A complete interpretive plan can also help to regulate tourists. If, for example, some places or ceremonies may be considered private and inappropriate for tourists, and locals always have a right to decide which sites and activities are open to the public. Tourists may be more sympathetic, however, if the reasons why they are not allowed to participate are clearly explained.

A successful tourism industry cannot be measured simply by the number of tourists; evidence has shown that an ever-increasing number of tourists is not necessarily a healthy tourism goal. If a community's physical and social limits, or "carrying capacity," are exceeded, the resulting conditions can cause a severe drop in economic (and other) benefits to the community. Interpretation can be a way of increasing tourist spending while discouraging many of the problems associated with mass tourism.

Many tourists are looking for more than a whirlwind trip to a large city or a few days on the beach. They want to have a sense of place, to understand the unique communities they are visiting. They are interested in other ways of life, and interpretation can help heighten this experience. However, these tourists consider themselves to be on vacation, not in school. They do not need to become experts—but would still like to learn something about the place they are enjoying.

Thoughtful interpretive programs offer the visitor a more meaningful experience than just a sunny beach or a nice view, and in the process, these programs reinforce and celebrate local heritage.

INTERPRETATION AND HERITAGE

In this chapter, *heritage* refers both to built and living culture: architectural styles and building practices, temples, colonial and new churches, archeological sites, festivals, myths, food preparation techniques, musical traditions, and unique ways of thinking and acting. Although the natural environment is an important part of every community—and its connections with both built and living culture should be acknowledged—this chapter focuses on cultural heritage. It is important to note, however, that the interpretive principles discussed here can also be applied to natural resources (e.g., parks, rivers, farms, and mountains).

This chapter discusses different ways to present a community and the story of its heritage. Resources such as brochures, walking trails, visitors' centers, festivals, and computer technology are all examples of ways to inspire tourists to return to learn and see more, and they are ways to support the local economy.

What Is Interpretation?

Two ways to communicate with visitors exist: in a factual style or in an interpretive style. The difference lies in how information is presented as opposed to what information is presented. An interpretive style reveals a story or a deeper message, whereas a factual style presents mostly facts.

The goal of interpretation is to change attitudes and behavior, to motivate and inspire, and to make information meaningful and exciting. Ultimately, this style of presenting information makes visitors more sensitive, aware, and understanding of a community's point of view.

The following is an example of the difference between factual and interpretive styles of communication:

A European woman touring a temple complex points at a Bodhi tree and asks her guide, "What kind of tree is that?"

Using a factual style, the guide would answer "A Bodhi tree," and leave it at that.

Using an interpretational style, he might say "This is a Bodhi tree. This species of tree is very important to Buddhists because the Buddha sat under a Bodhi tree as he achieved Nirvana, a state of enlightenment that is the ultimate goal of Buddhism in the way heaven is the ultimate goal of Christianity. We believe that every Bodhi tree is holy because it is connected to the original one. People often decorate the tree and offer incense to it as a Catholic might light a candle to a statue of a saint."

Which answer would the woman remember? Which one would spark her interest in the community she is visiting?

Interpretation is not just a glossy brochure, appropriate signage, and a well-edited video; it is the art of telling the story of a community.

This story is a collection of selected facts and experiences that can be given emotional and sensory meaning. All five senses can be used to enhance the experience of the visitor's environment. For example, the audience may be directed to feel the cool marble of a temple floor, smell a distillery or market, and hear the cries of street vendors. Too often we rely almost exclusively on the sense of sight when appreciating a new location even though we normally use all our senses in understanding an environment.

Good interpretation inspires further exploration. Once the main tourist area has been explored, the visitor may be directed on a self-guided tour to further explore the town. If problems occur in town planning, such as an attempt to repair a traditional building that was less than successful because too few people know the old carpentry techniques, they should not be glossed over, but rather pointed out. Discussing these problems with visitors will encourage them to care about a community's issues and possibly to help improve the community.

Any interpretation campaign, whether it features informed tour guides, illustrated booklets, written materials, films, visitor center displays, or signs at the site itself, should aim first to attract the visitor's attention, and secondly to inform, entertain, and stimulate in a comfortable and attractive setting.

Know the Audience

An important part of interpretation is the visitor's travel experiences with what is already familiar to him or her. The use of comparisons and background information will help the visitor identify with the message.

Often it will be necessary to interpret across cultures and deal with gaps in knowledge, so it is helpful to know something about who visitors are. Each part of the world has a different way of understanding family, religion, food, time, etc. For example, if most visitors to a community know a good deal about Buddhism, the interpretation for these tourists will be different than it would be for the average international tourist, who knows little about the same topic.

A familiar site may need to be reinterpreted to interest a local population. Schoolchildren touring a temple complex, for example, may be inspired and interested by stories about the lives of novice monks throughout the ages. A site can be endlessly reinterpreted because many stories and perspectives are available from which to view it.

However, each story should be consistent with the unique sense of place the community wants to convey.

Interpretation and Raising Local Awareness

Heritage education enhances civic pride and support for a site's preservation. It can also foster community-wide acceptance of tourism and the visitors it brings. Interpretation can be useful locally as well, to explain heritage to the general population and to local schoolchildren.

From the Bodhi tree example, it is clear how interpretation facilitates the learning process. It is important that consideration be given to the most effective and memorable ways to communicate the value of particular communities and sites to the public. This kind of awareness could help residents make better-informed decisions regarding their cultural environment. This is especially important for threatened architectural and archeological sites where increased support and awareness could improve chances for preservation. Community support can in turn encourage public and private sectors to financially support heritage preservation.

Resources Inventory

The first step a community should take is to research and make an inventory of its heritage resources. These resources may include historic buildings as well as everyday elements such as food preparation, a system of community land ownership, religious practices, and festival customs. The objective is to examine the fabric of the community closely to determine what stories to tell. If this inventory is omitted, a danger exists that the interpretation will focus only on the most obvious features, not on recognizing the special, but more subtle, qualities that give a community its distinctive sense of place. A methodical search of the area's physical and cultural features should be made, and areas not appropriate for tourists should be noted.

Subjects of Interpretation

The community resources and objectives will determine what story to tell. An important collection of historic buildings or a distinctive artistic tradition could be a major component of the story's theme. Good interpretation, however, can make even everyday resources interesting. In a project run by the Thai Volunteer Service, several villages in Thailand interpret daily life for visitors. Tourists grind corn, work the fields, pick fruit, and catch crabs. They learn cooking techniques and sources of traditional medicine. Where no important temples or archaeological sites exist, the village's resources are interpreted in a way that makes them interesting to visitors. The experience of spending a few days immersed in village life will stay with tourists far longer, and feel far more rewarding, than if they had spent their time looking at poorly interpreted temples.

If a community does not have a major attraction, imagination and brainstorming can help to discover what other elements of the community might be unique and interesting to outsiders. It may be surprising to hear that visitors from other countries are interested in the daily life of the communities they visit, but it is often true. Cooking methods and building methods, for example, may be very different from those in the visitor's home country. Presenting these aspects of heritage through interpretation creates a richer picture of the community. What local residents may consider boring, everyday life may be fascinating to tourists and unlike anything they have seen. Even if a community does have a major attraction, looking deeper to find other resources can lengthen a visitor's stay and enrich his or her experience.

Who Decides on Interpretation?

Different people will have different opinions about which heritage sites, living heritage resources, and artifacts are important as well as about how they should be interpreted. Experts in fields of architecture, history, or music may have interesting perspectives, but the local community should be able to decide how to interpret their own community for visitors. Conflicting ideas may exist within the community itself. A minority group, for example, may feel their contribution to the history and heritage of a community is undervalued. By working with experts and stakeholders who hold diverse views, however, all stakeholders can be represented, and a holistic vision of the community can be presented to visitors as well as to the local public.

Who Are the Visitors?

In order to interpret a community in a way visitors can relate to, it is important to keep track of who those visitors are. In fact, depending on how the interpretive program is planned, a community is actually able to control the types of tourists it attracts. The more information can be gathered about visitors, for example, where they come from and the motives and expectations of their visit, the more able planners will be to create programs and services that relate to visitors' needs and experiences.

Knowing the type of visitor helps to determine what kind of interpretive presentations will be used. If a large portion are older tourists on a bus tour, a long, self-guided walking trail would not be the most effective style of presentation. However, if most visitors are young, healthy backpackers, this type of trail would be ideal.

In many communities, statistics on tourism are not available, so alternative ways of information gathering may need to be developed. It is possible to evaluate the success of an interpretive program by asking local tour guides to survey tourists about what they learned and felt after visiting the community, and hotel owners can also get feedback from guests. If most tourists visit only for the day, talking to bus or ferryboat operators can help gather enough information to understand who is coming to the community and what kind of experience they are having. Not only does this information help with planning interpretation projects, it can contribute to the design of strategies to increase or change the type of tourists that come to a destination.

When developing a plan for community interpretation, tourists' needs for rest areas, shade, toilets, and safety as well as their interpretive requirements (how to interest and engage them in what they are seeing) must be considered.

A chronological theme could focus on a group of historical features or include a story about how historical figures responded to an event in a particular setting. The display and interpretation should unfold in a sequence of episodes, so that each episode communicates a complete notion on its own or can be linked to other events, past and present, to form the whole story.

Who Decides the Theme?

Outside pressures to develop a theme that may not seem appropriate to the local population often exist. National governments and commercial groups, such as tour companies, may want to choose a highly symbolic or political theme at the expense of popular forms of cultural expression of locally defined importance.

The United Nations Education, Scientific and Cultural Organization (UNESCO) World Heritage Site Luang Prabang in Lao People's Democratic Republic, for example, may represent the old Lanna kingdom to Thai visitors, the colonial era to French visitors, and may also hold deep religious significance for Laotians. The combination of these aspects contributes to Luang Prabang's sense of place, and interpretation may focus on the connections between these three different perspectives. Ultimately, however, the local community should decide what to present as most significant; the other topics can be discussed in terms of the decided theme.

Ideally, to ensure representation, all stakeholders should be consulted and should be able to participate in the interpretive planning process. The dangers of not taking control of the development of a community's theme are discussed in the following section.

PLANNING FOR INTERPRETATION

How and Why to Plan

In any community, the bottom line is that a well-thought-out plan is crucial to the creation of a sustainable and well-managed tourism industry. Interpretation is an important component of destination management, and should be part of a general tourism management plan. A separate, specific interpretive plan can help manage heritage resources, develop a marketing program, and serve as an example for other communities. It can also be important when looking for funding for an interpretive project.

Two ways to plan for interpretation exist. The most common is "defensive" planning: problems have already occurred, and planning is an attempt to fix them. However, it is generally better to plan ahead and anticipate what might go wrong after the plan has been implemented, such as changes in the types of visitors or in funding and budget, for example. This "offensive" planning includes allowing for room to expand existing interpretive services.

When devising a plan, the following elements should be considered:

- What are the resources, theme, and subtheme to be interpreted?
- Why are these resources and themes being presented to tourists, and what should the presentation accomplish?
- Who are visitors to the community? How can the theme be interpreted so they can understand and relate to it?
- How, when, and where are the interpretive program and services presented?
- What will it cost, in terms of people, time, resources, and budget, to implement the plan?
- How will the parts of the plan be evaluated to see if all objectives are achieved?

Mission Statement

A mission statement summarizes the overall goals of a project and should direct all interpretive services and programs. It is meant to be a general statement that sets out (1) who is organizing the project, (2) what the project aims to accomplish, and (3) why the project is important. It should reflect the individuality of the community and the goals of the specific interpretive program.

Objectives

A variety of goals may result from an interpretive program. The goal may be, for example, to raise funds to build a visitors' center, educate local schoolchildren, or increase the length of visitor stays, or it could be all three! These objectives are an important element of interpretive planning.

All objectives should be consistent with mission goals and must not undermine the principles and philosophy of the project. It may be necessary to adjust goals to fit the mission statement. Mass international tourism, for example, may not be a good goal for a village that aims to produce a unique and authentic experience of daily village life.

Evaluation

Objectives should be reevaluated constantly, annually at the very least. Implementing an interpretive program is of little use if it is not monitored regularly. It is important to find out what elements of the program visitors enjoy and why, and which ones do not achieve their interpretive goals. Were the times inconvenient? Was the trail too long? Was the visitor's center too hot to concentrate on the video? It may be necessary to modify the program accordingly. Interpretation style may need to be adjusted to achieve the project's goals and objectives, and checked to make sure objectives are reasonable.

If dependable statistics are not available, the informal techniques mentioned in the previous section (checking with hotel registers, tour operators, etc.) should provide some basic information.

The Possibilities

This section outlines some different ways to represent a community, keeping in mind that more than one mode of presentation can be used or several can be combined. For example, a map could accompany a walking trail, and a computer program could refer to that walking trail. Brochures could be distributed at a performance or be displayed outside the performance space.

Brochures

Brochures are the easiest and least expensive way to get information to a community's tourists. Even a simple brochure can provide information on where to go, what to see, and why those places and activities are significant to the community. Hotels, restaurants, tour companies, visitors' centers, and museums can distribute brochures. They can be designed to include different types of information, including guidelines for behavior and politeness. They can be tailored for specific events, such as festivals or dance performances, or even for an individual site. Brochures should illustrate and support the theme and objectives of an interpretive plan. Often a map and brochure are given out together, in which case the brochure can include interpretation, for example, for a self-guided trail.

Maps

Brochures and maps can accompany each other, or each can stand alone. Often, maps offer short explanatory interpretations of major sites on the reverse side. Maps can show highlights and heritage trail routes, and can include out-of-town destinations as well. Items left off the map are also important. Places not appropriate for tourists to visit, such as sacred sites, do not need to be on the map.

Heritage Trails

A walking trail is one of the most suitable interpretation tools for main commercial streets, cities, and towns. It presents the subject firsthand so that visitors are encouraged to explore the site for themselves. Subjects of the trail usually include buildings of historic interest, but interpretation should include information about planning, history, industry, and related social issues.

The Patan Tourism Development Organization in Patan, Nepal, created a self-guided walking tour that includes traditional houses, ponds, and squares as well as the impressive temples and palaces of the Durbar Square in Patan, part of the UNESCO World Heritage Site in the Kathmandu Valley. The tour describes the religious, social, and political forces that have affected the sites. The following is an excerpt from the walking tour brochure, distributed free with an entrance fee to historic Patan.

You will have already noticed how tall modern buildings affect the generally low, three-storied skyline of Patan. In the past, the height of the local temples tended to set the limit for residential buildings. The skyline, however, has changed rapidly in the last two decades due to several reasons: land values have greatly escalated; new building materials are now available; community controls have loosened; joint families have broken up, increasing the demand for separate dwellings; and the government is unable to enforce even the regulations that do exist. There are still quite a few streets, however, which retain their original integrity, whereas elsewhere the past has to be left to the imagination.

Audiovisual Interpretation

A presentation using sound and images is the most dramatic way to tell a story. Visitors seem to absorb more information from an audiovisual presentation than by reading about it. However, these types of media, such as videos and slide presentations, are also the most expensive.

A film or slide show can serve as an introduction to the site or provide most of the interpretive display. It can be copied and distributed to tourist or education centers as a way of attracting more visitors to the site.

Little India, the Indian district of Singapore, is a major tourist attraction in the city because of its restaurants, shops, festivals, and colorful population. The Singapore Tourism Board produced a video titled *Little India Through the Eyes of Dr. Uma Rajani* (a prominent local doctor). This film interprets Little India from the perspective of an insider, and takes place next to the food court in the Little India Arcade, where many tourists stop for lunch.

Interpretive Centers

A good interpretive center can offer valuable services to both a community and its visitors. It can provide the content of a museum, the entertainment of a themed attraction, and the services of a tourism information center. Visitors want to learn about the stories of a community, and an interpretive center can be an effective way to present this information.

An interpretive center need not be expensive. Depending on community resources it can be anything from an open-air shelter with a few wall-mounted display panels and maps to a multilevel air-conditioned museum.

Reasons to have an interpretive center include the following:

• To tell the story of the community
• To illustrate a story that cannot be told in-depth while on-site
• To show artifacts and tell stories
• To display and protect valuable artifacts
• To bring extremes into human scale
• To allow visitors to discover the story at their own pace
• To encourage visitors to further explore the community

- To meet the information needs of tourists
- To serve as a "home base" for tourists

The number of ways that themes can be illustrated is as plentiful as the number of existing interpretive centers. An interpretive center takes the themes and objectives outlined previously and concentrates them in one place. An interpretive center can be combined with a museum or information center along with the distribution of maps, guides, and brochures about local accommodations and restaurants. It can house commercial ventures, retail space for tour operators, or a café. It can serve as the starting point for a heritage trail. A window display can give a taste of the story inside or even highlight a local planning issue.

When planning for a center, objectives will need to be determined, just as they were for the community's interpretive plan. The following are some examples of goals for a center:

- All visitors will be encouraged to participate in the heritage tour that leaves from the interpretive center.
- All visitors will be made aware of the museum's programs and special community events.
- The majority of visitors will understand the main interpretive theme for the interpretive center exhibits.
- Specific learning, behavioral, and emotional goals will continue to be set.

If managers take some time to find out who the visitors will be, the center's displays and programs can be related to their background and experience. It will also be possible to determine if different presentation levels, such as a different language or interpretation for children, will need to be developed to target main visitor groups.

An outdoor covered exhibition, Ocean Art Works, was established at Granville Island Public Market in Vancouver, Canada, and sponsored by a nearby concrete company. The vibrant market and artistic community make the site both a produce market for locals and a tourist attraction.

This artists' space is roofed but open on three sides. First Nations carvers have used the space to craft totem poles, wooden canoes, and other sculptures. One pole may take several months to complete. The carving process is an attraction to the hundreds of people that walk past every day. The advantage of this type of space is that the carving process is accessibly displayed instead of being hidden away in a studio.

The art and designs of First Nations culture are featured all over Vancouver and even figure prominently at the international airport. This Granville Island space allows for demonstrations of the living culture of an important cultural group in Vancouver, whose symbols are everywhere but whose living culture is not often accessible to residents or visitors.

Museums

Converting an existing heritage building into a visitors' center creates historical ambience. Often an old building such as a town hall, post office, or railway building can be converted into a museum or interpretive center. The cost of purchasing a building may be avoided if the property is not currently a viable commercial building; the owner may agree to a long-term lease at a low rent or may be willing to sell for a nominal fee. Local governments often own some of these properties. If the building is declared a historic site, some funding may be available from national governments.

The Museum of Macao in Macao, China, incorporates the past and present throughout the building. Outdoor escalators take advantage of Macao's pleasant climate. Inside, the facades of old buildings, both in Western and Chinese style, are reconstructed on an almost full-size scale. The museum is also built so that, upon leaving, the visitors are able to see a view of modern Macao and place the museum within its broader context.

Funding and Organization

Many communities think they do not have the money to develop any sort of interpretive center. However, by looking beyond municipal and other public coffers, a broad array of funding sources can be found. One of the most lucrative partnerships can be made between the public and private sectors.

Two major components in the financing of an interpretive facility exist: capital and daily operating costs (including costs for updating exhibits).

CONCLUSION

In this chapter, many different formats for presenting a community's heritage have been outlined. A host of other options are also available, limited only by a community's resourcefulness and imagination. A well-planned and appealing interpretation program can have far-reaching positive implications for a community's sustainable tourism. The essence of good interpretation, however, requires the community itself, in all its complexity, to define the themes and resources of interpretation and decide how its people and heritage should be represented.

BIBLIOGRAPHY

Canadian Universities Consortium-Asian Institute of Technology (CUC-AIT). 2000. *Tourism Plan for Phimai, Thailand.* Bangkok, Thailand: Canadian Universities Consortium Urban Environmental Management Project.

Hatton, M.J. 1999. *Community-Based Tourism in the Asia Pacific.* Singapore: Asia Pacific Economic Cooperation.

Nuryanti, W. 1997. Interpreting heritage for tourism: Complexities and contradictions. In W. Nuryanti (Ed.), *Tourism and Heritage Management.* Yogyakarta, Indonesia: Gadjah Mada University Press.

United Nations Education, Scientific and Cultural Organization (UNESCO). 1993. *Case Study on the Effects of Tourism on Culture and the Environment, India.* Bangkok, Thailand: UNESCO.

UNESCO. 1995. *World Heritage: Ours Forever? Treasures of the Asia-Pacific Region.* Bangkok, Thailand: UNESCO.

Veverka, J.A. 1994. *Interpretive Master Planning.* Helena, MT: Falcon Press.

Vines, E. 1996. *Streetwise—A Practical Guide.* Adelaide, Australia: National Trust of Australia.

Chapter 7

GIS, Remote Sensing, and Tourism Destination Management

Richard M. Levy
Elizabeth E. Dickson

Geographic information systems and remote sensing are becoming critical tools for tourism destination management planning. The ability to access and analyze spatial data will help to coordinate the activities of governments, tour operators, hotel owners, and other community members motivated to capture the promised benefits of tourism.

INTRODUCTION

Improvements in Geographic information systems (GIS) and remote sensing (RS) technologies have greatly increased the availability of spatial data over the past 15 years. These easily analyzed and displayed images and digital databases of biophysical information have transformed our world perspective. Universal access to spatially referenced databases within a GIS has given governments, nongovernmental organizations, corporations, and individuals a valuable knowledge base for making critical decisions and formulating long-range plans. Through their ability to capture images of the physical environment from any location in the world, remote sensors mounted on satellites, airplanes, and helicopters have provided a means to monitor changes to the landscape. The rapid adoption of GIS and RS promises to create a shared virtual world that can be used to examine

Community Destination Management in Developing Economies
© 2006 by The Haworth Press, Inc. All rights reserved.
doi:10.1300/5140_08

a broad range of economic and physical planning questions (Entwisle et al., 1998; Chen et al., 2000). GIS and RS are now seen as essential tools for the destination management process. This chapter will examine specific dimensions of how GIS and RS are important components of the overall destination management process.

GIS and RS: Tools for Managing Change

GIS and RS are digital planning tools to manage and coordinate tourism-related development on both local and regional scales. This chapter first provides a brief introduction to GIS and RS technology, then discusses their applications to tourism destination management.

Geographic Information Systems

GIS is "a system of computer hardware, software and procedures designed to support the capture, management, manipulation, analysis, modullary and display of spatially referenced data for solving complex management and planning problems" (Federal Interagency Coordinating Committee 1988, cited in Antenucci et al., 1991, p. 7). GIS grew out of a desire to link the graphic design tools of engineers with the databases of planners, economists, and scientists. Within a GIS data can be displayed and examined in a spatial framework. Land feature information can be grouped or layered using an organizing theme, such as hydrology or roads.

Beyond simple mapping, GIS is a powerful analytic tool, useful for uncovering the connections between classes of objects using modeling techniques (Berry, 1993). Within a GIS, spatial attributes can be inputs to simulation models aimed at predicting economic, ecological, or global processes. In this way, the effects of different planning scenarios on the local ecology (e.g., forest fragmentation or bird habitat in wetlands) or urban systems (e.g., transportation networks or telecommunication structures) can be tested before implementation. When remotely sensed image data is layered within a GIS, survey features (e.g., roads, canals, and buildings) can be correlated with the landscape as viewed from overhead. Fragmentation of sensitive habitat and damage from floods, fire, or pollution can be measured and evaluated using this overlay approach (Zhou et al., 2000).

The core of all GIS is data. Data for a GIS may be gathered through field studies or acquired from the private sector and government agencies in raw format, such as tables or maps, and also in digital format. GIS data includes spatially explicit information (where the feature is located) as well as attribute information (the feature's properties and characteristics) (see Table 7.1).

Remote Sensing

With the growth of RS technology, planners can observe change from a vantage point far above the earth (Lillisand and Keifer, 1994). Traditionally, single images of the earth's surface have been captured from cameras mounted on airplanes with panchromatic (black and white) or color film. With the development of satellite and imaging technology, digital images covering the entire earth became available from space, first to military and governmental agencies and later to the scientific and general public. Remote sensors continue to improve, providing images with higher spectral and spatial resolution than previously possible. For example, early Landsat satellite images (1972-1982) consisted of four multispectral bands with 80 megapixel spatial resolution. Landsat satellite images from 1982 to 2001 consist of seven multispectral bands (30 meters per pixel). Since the launch of Landsat 7 in 2000, an additional panchromatic band (15 meters per pixel) has been available. In 2000, IKONOS satellite imagery became obtainable with four multispectral bands (4 megapixels) and a panchromatic band (1 megapixel)—a level of detail comparable in spatial resolution to aerial photography.

TABLE 7.1. Examples of GIS data.

Feature/Theme	Attributes
Roads	Intersections, direction, number of lanes
City land use and zoning	Permitted uses, current use
Demographics	Age by cohort, ethnicity, income
Soils	Texture, parent material, drainage
Terrain	Elevation, slope, aspect
Land cover	Vegetation (forest, brush, grassland), lakes, rivers, urban development

Scale and Resolution

Spatially based, GIS and RS analyses are sensitive to issues of scale. When developing a system to answer specific questions about the built and natural environment, time frame, geographic extent, and spatial resolution are all important considerations. For example, image scale and resolution determine the type and detail of features that can be extracted out of remotely sensed data. If relatively small features, such as individual houses, are the objects of interest, the spatial resolution of the imagery will need to be higher than if larger features, such as land covers, are the targeted objects. In addition to spatial resolution, spectral resolution affects what features are identified, particularly those associated with specific wavelength reflectance intensities. When these associations are distinctive, the spectral resolution of a sensor determines whether characteristic objects (e.g., certain vegetation and mineral types) are detected. For GIS and RS analyses, the spectral and spatial requirements of a particular project should ideally drive the data selection.

TOURISM DESTINATION MANAGEMENT AND BUILDING CONSENSUS

GIS can enable communities to develop strategies for tourism destination management within a framework of public participation. The provision of data in map form means that a common basis for understanding past development and future options can be shared among all participants involved in the planning process. Properly used, GIS can create a sense of immediacy and a commitment to shared community concerns among all stakeholders (Barndt, 1994; Kyem, 1998). For example, for locals in Ghana concerned with forestry, skepticism disappeared after their introduction to GIS (Kyem, 1998). By creating an information portal unfiltered by planners and government officials, a reliable source of historical and current data is more universally available. By offering members of the community, businesses engaged in tourism, and government officials access to data comparisons across time and space, a shared framework for decision support can be built (Collins, 1998). Aspects of public participation that GIS can enhance include the following:

- *Building trust.* If data can be viewed as unbiased and independent of the political process, trust can be built among stakeholders.
- *Leveling the playing field.* Access to a common database can make everyone more equal in the political process.
- *Providing a common vision.* GIS establishes a common framework for understanding biophysical, economic, demographic, and other related spatial data. Having a free and open database can help establish common understanding by preserving agreements made during the course of discussions among stakeholders. Future negotiations can be based on a common foundation.
- *Supporting differentiated knowledge about a community.* Rather than supporting a single viewpoint, GIS can serve a variety of interest groups by fostering sensitivity to the needs of different groups such as women, the elderly, and children.
- *Promoting shared solutions.* A common database allows all parties to share solutions and resolve conflicts. Though all negotiations must acknowledge differences of opinion, when the focus is on finding solutions, discussions can be advanced beyond the viewpoint of a single stakeholder (Kyem, 1998).
- *Providing the basis for comparison across communities.* Building a comprehensive database can encourage regional solutions. By identifying shared resources, such as water management, air pollution, and transportation planning, jurisdictions with common concerns are encouraged to work together to find common solutions.
- *Encouraging scenario- and model-building.* Scenarios and models can be compared without concern that differences in data are responsible for contradictory projections.
- *Establishing a historical record.* Preservation of the historical record in a shared database will discourage the rewriting of history to suit the political process. Historical records can also serve as a basis for public education and a repository for local knowledge. Stakeholders are no longer dependent on institutional memory for knowledge about the past.
- *Using scarce resources wisely.* The sharing of data among government agencies, local jurisdictions, community groups, and the private sector reduces the need to duplicate data collection.

Time and resources can be devoted to analysis rather than to data collection.

- *Releasing constraints of time and distance.* Internet communication makes the sharing of data across time and distance possible (Al-Kodmany, 1998; Howard, 1998; Kyem, 1998; Forester, 1989).

HISTORIC RESOURCE MANAGEMENT

GIS has multiple uses for historic resource management. Throughout more than two decades of work in archaeology, GIS and RS technology have shown themselves to be powerful forces in the location, interpretation, and preservation of historic sites. RADARSAT, Landsat TM, and air photo images over vast regions have been critical to the location of previously unknown temples, cities, and fortifications. The discovery of many temple sites in Angkor and China was possible only through the use of radar imagery, which can reveal changes in topography even in areas persistently under cloud cover.

These surveys have created a more complete model of the past. The discovery of ancient roads, canals, and irrigation systems using remotely sensed data has expanded our knowledge of the intricacies of human settlement. With the encroachment of human activity into areas once remote, the potential destruction of these important historic sites is more probable than in the past. Extensive inventories can aid governments in the protection of these culturally significant sites (Lock and Zoran, 1995; Box, 1999; Gilman, 1999; Kvamme, 1999; Fowler, 2000).

At the other extreme of scale, single temple sites can be imaged using laser technology capable of preserving detail as small as 0.2 mm. Combined with digital photography, it is possible to create virtual copies of entire buildings and sites (Forstner and Gulch, 1999). GIS could be used by scholars, archaeologists, teachers, and students around the world to establish an information system that integrates text, plans, maps, images, video, and other multimedia content. Ultimately this database could serve as the basis for virtual tourism, allowing anyone with access to the Internet to explore (for example) a vast temple complex. Virtual tourism is already emerging as an important development in promotion and education of a public with a growing interest in the arts. (For an example of three-dimensional-imaging technology that was used to document cultural resources, see Geo Insight International, Inc., 2005.)

For those government agencies involved in preservation and management, virtual models can be an important tool in the monitoring of change. A critical component in the plan to develop tourism in the region will be the protection of temples and sacred sites. Without proper management, certain historic sites could face considerable damage from the tourists who will visit over the coming years. Constant wear from continued use of these fragile sites can only result in severe physical deterioration. Under high-use circumstances, restoration and preservation should be ongoing processes. An information system to monitor activities is crucial to the future preservation of the many important historic and archaeological sites (Geo Insight International, Inc., 2005).

Information acquired in support of preservation activities can also be used to create a database to support tourism development. An information portal built on top of a GIS can add a new dimension to the tourist's search for information about a destination. Planning an itinerary complete with accommodations, tours, transportation, and events can be accomplished via two-way communication between operators and tourists. Ultimately, preplanning services over the Internet can provide the tourist and the business traveler with a level of assurance about his or her itinerary, translating into a larger share of the world tourism market for that region.

GIS/RS AND BIOPHYSICAL PLANNING ISSUES

Understanding landscape issues at the regional scale will help communities and governments monitor the impact of human settlement on the environment. Building an inventory of topography, hydrology, land cover, and land use is the first step in establishing a baseline for biophysical attributes. Information extracted from the images can be correlated with field data. Ultimately, classifications by land use or type (e.g., forest, cropland, urban) are needed to support the decision makers and planners. For example, an ecological study might require information about vegetation composition and wetland location, whereas a tourism study might require information about beach locations and pollution sources.

In the past, manual interpretation of aerial photographs has been the primary source of this information. Human recognition of ground objects was determined from their tone, texture, brightness, and shape. In contrast to a single black and white (panchromatic) or color air photography print, multispectral imagery can consist of many layers of data. One automated approach for extracting information is to perform a multivariate analysis in order to classify regions together that share similar reflectance patterns. Computer algorithms for classification also are available that rely on the image analyst to first define the spectral composition of classes. Today, with advances in computing, it is possible to employ more advanced techniques such as fuzzy logic, decision trees, and ancillary data to classify image data. Once classified, planners can integrate remotely sensed data into a GIS for use as a decision support tool (Gong and Haworth, 1990; Cowen and Jensen, 1998; Coulter et al., 1999; Jensen and Cowen, 1999).

GIS can help communities understand the complex relationship between development and the preservation of ecosystems. This knowledge can be critical in the development of a new project for which the proximity to natural amenities must be balanced against the cost of improving existing infrastructure. For resorts located in areas outside of major urban centers, the acquisition of water, sewer, gas, electricity, phone, and roads can prove very costly. Having a GIS can help in the estimation of these improvement expenses. Other site preparation costs, such as laying foundations and landscaping, can also be estimated for each location under consideration. But as important as it is to estimate the cost of improvements, an examination must also be made of the impact of development on the local environment (McAdam, 1999).

If a region is to prosper through tourism, the expansion of resort development must not damage the natural beauty of the area. GIS can play a key role in our development of an understanding of the effects of human activity upon an environment (Entwisle et al., 1998; Buckley, 1999). By establishing a biophysical baseline, it is possible to measure the impacts of development on sensitive habitat and water quality. A comprehensive information structure allows groups with conflicting goals to consider solutions that would benefit all parties.

For example, in areas that are involved in both tourism and forestry, cutting trees close to streams or in tourists' view can have a negative impact on sport fishing, bathing areas, water quality, and aesthetic appeal, making the area less attractive for tourism. Similarly, the construction of hotels without adequate provision for water, sewer, and waste collection can also result in the pollution of the local water table. Many beach communities, after years of uncontrolled dumping of trash and sewage, face the loss of future revenue from tourism. In these cases, pollution has destroyed a valuable community asset.

Scenic beauty and other visual features are also important to protect. Unless considered during the planning stage, the construction of new facilities can block views of important topographical features or contrast starkly with vernacular architecture. GIS can provide both the private and public sector with a means to preview the impact of development on the natural and urban environments. Rather than focusing on isolated developments, GIS can foster a more comprehensive approach in which destination planning and management has a mandate to safeguard both the environment and future tourism.

CONCLUSION: GIS AND DECISION SUPPORT

Immediate access to data is an obvious benefit of GIS. Enhanced work flow, improvement in reporting capability, and greater ease of response to daily inquiries are some of the less visible operational benefits of GIS. Most important, GIS enhances the ability to make timely decisions based on accurate information, which, in turn, greatly assists council and municipal officials in their duties. The goal of GIS in the context of tourism destination management is to provide guidance for the creation of a comprehensive system that can organize and unify information currently maintained on independent systems. Another aim of these information networks should be to provide a medium through which people at different locations can more easily share data and tourism planning ideas. Many inquiries require access to spatial data, and another benefit of a GIS environment is to improve the management of current operations in both the public and private sectors. However, many obstacles to the establishment of a universally accessible GIS still exist. Extensive investments in hardware, software, data, applications development, and technical training need to be made. The creation of universal access to data and the process of planning requires the shared responsibility and commitment of both the private and public sectors.

REFERENCES

Al-Kodmany, K. 1998. *GIS and the Artist: Shaping the Image of a Neighborhood in Participatory Environmental Design*. Paper prepared for the Project Varenius specialist Meeting on Empowerment, Marginalization and Public Participation, October, 1998. Santa Barbara, California. Available online at: http://www.ncgia. ucsb.edu/varenius/ppgis/papers/al-kodmany.html.

Alzua, A., J.T. O'Leary, and A.M. Morrison. 1998. Cultural and heritage tourism: Identifying niches for international travelers. *The Journal of Tourism Studies* 9(2): 2-13.

Antenucci, J., K. Brown, P. Crosell, and M. Kevany. 1991. *Geographic Information Systems*. New York: Van Nostrand Reinhold.

Barndt, M.G. 1994. Data providers empower community GIS efforts. *GIS World* 7: 49-51.

Berry, J. 1993. *Beyond Mapping: Concepts, Algorithms and Issues in GIS*. Fort Collins, CO: GIS World Books.

Box, P. 1999. *An Introduction to the Use of Geographical Information Systems (GIS) in Heritage Management: A Manual for Heritage Managers*. UNESCO.

Buckley, R. 1999. Tourism and biodiversity: Land-use, planning and impact assessment. *The Journal of Tourism Studies* 10(2): 47-56.

Chen, S., S. Zeng, and C. Xie. 2000. Remote sensing and GIS for urban growth analysis in China. *Photogrammetric Engineering & Remote Sensing* 66(5): 593-598.

Collins, B. 1998. Land use planning on the Web. *GIS Asia Pacific* 8: 46-48.

Coulter, L., D. Stow, B. Kiracofe, C. Langevin, D. Chen, S. Daeschner, D. Service, and J. Kaiser. 1999. Deriving current land-use information for metropolitan transportation planning through integration of remotely sensed data and GIS. *Photogrammetric Engineering & Remote Sensing* 65(11): 1293-1300.

Cowen, D. and J. Jensen. 1998. Extraction and modeling on urban attributes using remote sensing technology. In D. Liverman, E. Barron, P. Epstein, B. McKay, E. Moran, E. Parson, R. Rindfuss, V. Rutton, R. Socolow, J. Sweeney, et al. (Eds.), *People and Pixels: Linking Remote Sensing and Social Science* (pp. 164-188). Washington, DC: National Academy Press.

Entwisle, B., S. Walsh, R. Rindfuss, and A. Chamratrithirong. 1998. Land-use/land-cover and population dynamics, Nang Rong, Thailand. In D. Liverman, E. Barron, P. Epstein, B. McKay, E. Moran, E. Parson, R. Rindfuss, V. Rutton, R. Socolow, J. Sweeney, et al. (Eds.), *People and Pixels: Linking Remote Sensing and Social Science* (pp. 121-144). Washington, DC: National Academy Press.

Forester, J. 1989. *Planning in the Face of Power*. Berkeley, CA: University of California Press.

Forstner, W. and W. Gulch. 1999. Automatic orientation and recognition in highly structured scenes. *Photogrammetric Engineering & Remote Sensing* 54(1): 23-34.

Fowler, M. 2000. In search of history. *Space Imaging* 15(6): 18-21.

Geo Insight International, Inc. 2005. *Cultural Resource Documentation Using Cyra Technology.* Available online at: http://www.geoinsight.com/Knowledgebase/CulturalResourcesCyra/Cultural_Resource.pdf.

Gilman, P. 1999. Securing a future for Essex's past. *ArcUsers* 2(4): 30-33.

Gong, P. and P. Howarth. 1990. The use of structural information for improving land-cover classification accuracies at the rural-urban fringe. *Photogrammetric Engineering & Remote Sensing* 56(1): 67-73.

Haack, B., D. Craven, and J. McDonald. 1996. GIS tracks Kathmandu Valley's urban explosion. *GIS World* 2: 54-57.

Howard, D. 1998. *Geographic Information Technologies and Community Planning: Spatial Empowerment.* Available online at: http://www.ncgia.ucsb.edu/varenius/ppgis/papers/howard.html.

Jensen, J. and D. Cowen. 1999. Remote sensing of urban/suburban infrastructure and socio-economic attributes. *Photogrammetric Engineering & Remote Sensing* 65(5): 611-622.

Koirala, H.L. 1998. *RS and GIS in Assessing Urban Environment: A Case Study of Kathmandu Metropolitan City, Kathmandu Valley.* Formerly available online at: http://pages.hotbot.com/edu/geoinformatics/f118.html.

Kvamme, K. 1999. Recent directions and developments in geographic information systems. *Journal of Archaeology Research* 7(2): 153-201.

Kyem, P. 1998. *Promoting Local Community Participation in Forest Management through the Application of a Geographic Information System: A PPGIS Experience from Southern Ghana.* Paper prepared for the Project Varenius Specialist Meeting on Empowerment, Marginalization and Public Participation, October, 1998. Santa Barbara, California. Available online at: http://www.ncgia.ucsb.edu/varenius/ppgis/papers/kyem/kyem.html.

Lillisand, T.M. and R.W. Kiefer. 1994. *Remote Sensing and Image Interpretation.* New York: John Wiley and Sons, Inc.

Lock, G. and S. Zoran. 1995. *Archaeology and Geographical Information Systems.* London: Taylor and Francis.

McAdam, D. 1999. The value and scope of Geographical Information Systems in tourism management. *Journal of Sustainable Tourism* 7(1): 77-92.

Travel Industry Publishing. 2000. *The Travel Industry World 2000 Yearbook: The Big Picture.* Spencertown, NY: Travel Industry Publishing Company.

Zhou, C., J. Lou, C. Yang, B. Li, and S. Wang. 2000. Flood monitoring using multitemporal AVHRR and RADARSAT imagery. *Photogrammetric Engineering & Remote Sensing* 65(5): 633-683.

Chapter 8

Good Governance
in Destination Management

Willi Zimmermann

INTRODUCTION

It is often assumed that the primary goal of tourism destination planning and management is to increase the number of tourist arrivals. Thus, many projects focus on promotion in the client market and neglect the communities that host tourists. However, unbridled, unmanaged growth can do irreparable harm to local societies and their environment, jeopardizing the sector's own development potential. Burgeoning tourism eats up space, and the influx of tourists puts extra pressure on the natural environment, bringing about major changes in the local culture.

In the decades ahead, tourism, the world's largest industry, is set to continue to expand in both developed and developing countries. Competition will become more intense, and a risk exists that tourism will have adverse impacts. If not kept in check, tourism can damage the environment—destroying nature reserves, threatening biodiversity, polluting water, and producing waste. It can also do harm to a community's cultural and social fabric, potentially leading to job insecurity, deteriorating working conditions, prostitution, threats to human rights, the impoverishment of culture and traditions, overexploitation, and a consequent degradation of cultural sites.

This chapter was prepared with the assistance of Beatriz Mayer when she was a research associate at the Asian Institute of Technology, Thailand.

Community Destination Management in Developing Economies
© 2006 by The Haworth Press, Inc. All rights reserved.
doi:10.1300/5140_09

To promote economic growth while ensuring its compatibility with the protection of the environment as well as to uphold human rights and safeguard the country's social fabric are key objectives to be pursued in the development of tourism in all countries. Maintaining a tourist destination and its environment on a long-term basis requires the involvement of authorities, the host community, and private entrepreneurs. It calls for the tourism industry to seek active collaboration with environmental organizations and communities in the preservation and restoration of the environment.

The Concept of Good Governance

The concept of *governance,* often used in discussions concerning improving the situation of developing countries, takes many different forms. Some authors speak of "corporate governance," others simply of "governance," and elsewhere "good governance" is the talk of the town. The Chartered Institute of Public Finance and Accountancy in London defined in its document *Corporate Governance: A Framework for Public Service Bodies* (1995) three areas that are relevant for governance:

1. Board/top policymaking structure and organization
2. Financial reporting and internal control processes
3. Standards of personal behavior and integrity

The Canadian Institute On Governance has defined governance as the ways in which government and other social organizations interact, relate to citizens, and make decisions in an increasingly complex world. According to several United Nations Development Programme (UNDP) documents, good governance includes participation, the rule of law, transparency, responsiveness, consensus orientation, equity, effectiveness and efficiency, accountability, and strategic vision.

Although this definition is quite far-reaching, it will nevertheless be used throughout the article for its useful implication that state and administration are not the only players in the realization of the common good, and that others must be involved as well.

The Concept of Participation

The democratizing forces that emerged in most of the developing world in the late 1980s and the 1990s expanded the scope and meaning of *participation*. These movements saw the reemergence of the civil society as a complement to the state and the market in charting the course of development. The concept of participation was further conceptualized in the United Nations Conference on the Environment and Development at Rio de Janeiro in 1992. The conference officially stated that challenges of development called for the active collaboration between governments, the private sector, and the public.

Participation can help build long-term capacity and improve the ability of local communities to manage and influence the outcome of their development. Participation should aim to reconcile economic development with the broader interests of the host community and the potential effects of tourism on the community's environment. Consultation between the government sector, private sector, and local community is essential to the planning of a development project that minimizes negative effects and maximizes benefits (Eber, 1992).

The local community's level of participation can vary. Generally, public participation is defined as a two-way communication process that encourages a full public understanding of the different dimensions of tourism. It can range from information gathering or planned communication to education of communities and more active forms of participation, such as taking part in direct decision-making, planning, development, services delivery, and ownership. The following list shows levels of citizen participation (Arnstein, 1969):

Degrees of Citizen Power	Degrees of tokenism	Nonparticipation
Citizen control	Placation	Therapy
Delegated power	Consultation	Manipulation
Partnerships	Informing	

However, the goal of public participation should not be only to keep the local community informed but to actively require its opinions and participation as well. Projects imposed on the community often neglect local interest. Lack of cooperation with local communities can be the cause of opposition, conflict, and eventual failure. In fact, equality in participation is necessary to project success.

Equality in Public Participation

Equality in public participation must satisfy the following three conditions:

1. A high degree of citizen involvement (both in numbers and in extent of individual participation)
2. Equity in participation (each different group or sector should be equally represented)
3. Efficiency in participation (the ratio between the resources invested in managing public participation and the output should be practical) (Simmons, 1994)

These different conditions are not always entirely compatible, and tensions can arise. One of the main concerns about participatory approaches is that they consume time and resources, which can pose a significant challenge to a project. However, although the early stages (planning) may be slower, once a compromise has been found the implementation can be correspondingly easier and faster. In addition, poorly targeted participatory schemes may promote a certain ideological perspective in development that will limit the number of groups to be included in any discussions and the range of solutions and policies that will be considered.

To achieve citizen involvement, equity, and efficiency, well-defined participatory techniques and clear motivation for participatory approaches must be chosen. Different techniques will address different objectives and stages of development, from theoretical levels of policy and vision to more practical, operational levels.

Participation mechanisms must be chosen to match the expected output of public participation. They should also be related to the stage of planning and the extensiveness of the plan. Thus, local communities can involve themselves directly in planning, decision making, and implementation through representatives in committees and in workshops—and can be indirectly involved in planning through public meetings and surveys.

PUBLIC PARTICIPATION
IN TOURISM MANAGEMENT

In general, since the creation of modern tourism in the 1950s, tourism management has evolved through three stages, with a fourth stage now emerging (Go, 1993). The realization that residents' attitudes toward tourism is one of the key elements in achieving sustainable tourism—and that active community involvement is therefore fundamental to development planning—is the basis of the most recent developmental stage in tourism management.

> *Stage I: Product.* Development (in terms of infrastructure) of a site that will automatically attract tourists
> *Stage II: Sales.* Hard-sale stage
> *Stage III: Marketing.* Bringing together sales profits and consumer orientation ("desire to please" as a tourist commodity)
> *Stage IV: Social responsibility.* Organizations place greater emphasis on socially responsible action, demonstrating concern for their stakeholders, among them customers, travel industry partners, and host communities. During the 1980s, tourism began to pay attention to the resources that sustain it. A region's residents are increasingly being considered as part of the tourism resources.

This latest shift focuses on the relationship between tourism, tourists, and host communities, and recognizes that under certain conditions it can be a win-win situation for all parties. The lack of public participation can prove harmful for local people, leading to the damage of natural resources or to the abandonment of traditional occupations and lifestyles—clearly, a loss to locals as well as to tourists. On the other hand, maximizing benefits to local residents can result in the active collaboration of communities and in active support for conservation of local tourism resources.

For example, participation in tourism planning and management educates the community about the potential long-term benefits of tourism. This is a very important step to promote tourism. A proper integration of community objectives and tourism should be the following:

- *Democratic.* Including the right of participation for anyone interested in doing so, as well as encouraging them to do so
- *Integrative.* Representing different groups and hence reflecting the expectations of the overall local communities, even at the risk of conflict emergence
- *Systematic.* Extending through all the stages of the development and implementing regular mechanisms for ongoing support, with periodic survey on community attitudes and satisfaction
- *Goal-oriented.* Developing a community tourism vision of desired future state, incorporating a community's belief and values (Simmons, 1994)

The World Tourism Organization (1994) has stressed these points of view, especially in the context of sustainable tourism, and has pointed out that tourism development should reflect a consensus of wishes and expectations. Local residents will support tourism if they are involved in its planning and development and are made aware of potential benefits and risks. Their support and involvement from a very early stage of planning, development, and management are fundamental to the achievement of sustainable development. Committing this support demands the following:

- Involvement of the community through consultation early in the process
- Encouragement of cooperation and linkages between the citizens and the tourism effort
- Ongoing education and communication as well as consultation with the community about tourism in the area (CUC UEM TTTP, 1999)

Community Involvement Through Early-Stage Consultation

From its earliest stages, planning must involve the different groups affected by the tourism development project. The lack of stakeholder participation is one of the main causes of project failure. The community should be involved at all stages, but the planning stage is especially crucial. This approach intends to develop the type of tourism that generates benefits to local communities. It stresses, especially, the need to ensure that benefits remain mostly in the community, not with outsiders.

Encouraging Cooperation Between Citizens and the Tourism Effort

The World Tourism Organization (1994) also recommends that a steering committee, at the national and regional level, composed of representatives of government agencies, the private sector, and community organizations should encourage public involvement through public hearings or tourism seminars that would offer guidance to the planning team and would review plans.

Continued Education, Communication, and Consultation with the Community

Residents—shopkeepers, owners, managers of restaurants and hotels, etc.—need to be encouraged to learn and master the skills required to manage special tourist sites, including natural, historic, cultural, or folkloric settings. At the same time, education and consultation programs for tourism in the area help the host community understand the pros and cons of tourism and prepares the community to accept its role as host and assist and welcome visitors. However, this approach can fail when it is done superficially, without recognizing the individual characteristics of the host community.

These recommendations from the World Tourism Organization should now be taken a few steps further. In many countries, especially developing countries, tourism takes place in a weak institutional framework. Given the powerful players with strong self-interests, such as airlines, tour operators, hotel chains who will also be jostling for influence, vigorous administration and planning are also vital. Without these two resources it will be difficult to monitor and control the positive and negative repercussions of tourism.

Sustainable tourism destination management requires good governance. This involves the following:

- The intervention of public authorities, who must set up a legal and institutional framework: legislation, policies, rules and regulations for participation, monitoring, jurisdiction, etc.
- Coordination between all parties. Since different public bodies have to share responsibilities, avoiding unbalanced growth and

unnecessary competition requires that public authorities provide a structured and ongoing dialogue between all the partners.

- Involvement of all the players, and backing of initiatives by regional authorities and municipalities. Tourism development consonant with principles of decentralized cooperation involves the economic and social players and strengthens the role of civil society associations. This often requires:
  —Enhancing the know-how of local administrations
  —Supporting local initiatives that embrace the various aspects of tourism development
  —Consolidating the role of civil society
- The ability of public authorities to carry out strategic planning and, where necessary, human resources development (at all local levels). This type of planning fixes clear targets and objectives and insists on measuring performance. Since the planning stage is the earliest and often the most complex and tiresome, it may be useful to stress the participatory elements.

PLANNING PRINCIPLES

On the host community level, effective tourism management requires an understanding of how tourism works as well as how to apply management techniques effectively to achieve the desired results (Simmons, 1994). Participatory approaches aid tourism development in the host community by doing the following:

- Helping to determine what communities can gain from the tourism process. This is achieved by identifying economic, social, and labor force needs for tourism, analyzing the community's and region's current level of involvement in tourism, and comparing it with other existing economic sectors through an examination of existing economic and tourism planning and development documents (local and regional).
- Identifying the type of tourism that would complement the local way of life as perceived desirable by the local community, based on the community's attitudes, concerns, interests, and values. It is important to present the potential positive and negative changes that tourism will cause in the community.

- Empowering local people to take up the leadership challenge and be adaptable to change. Leadership for the tourism process is established by identifying key leaders (formal and informal) and key groups (main stakeholders), appointing a community tourism organization, and establishing planning scope. Leadership should also be translated into community involvement with financial planning to facilitate the understanding of investment opportunities for local businesses.
- Demonstrating how to manage special places, to optimize positive impacts, and to avoid negative impacts through a learning process. Communities looking to enhance their tourism flows must first assess their own identities, lifestyles, and environment, recognizing and enriching their natural and cultural assets. For that, appointed facilitators should identify key community themes, issues, and concerns related to tourism, and formulate a work plan and process for broad-based community input.
- Establishing linkages between communities and experts to build organizational capability and to build community awareness and information exchange programs through proper communication policies. The community's attitudes and satisfaction should be periodically surveyed. Consultation and conflict resolution processes should be put in place, and education programs should be developed to enable local communities to recognize and maintain the value of their cultural and social heritage.

CONCLUSION

Sustainable tourism management requires the involvement of communities, both in the planning process and in the implementation of action plans. The benefits of this approach have been widely acknowledged. Wide participation benefits the host community economically, and also promotes cultural exchange and enriches the learning experience of both tourists and hosts.

Real integration of the community should involve local residents beyond those directly participating in the developments. Real integration also requires a deep and compromising participation, ruling out the sole use of consultation, and stressing the use of more empowering participatory measures that give a factual influence to the communities. Despite the complexities, participation approaches for local communities are an emerging force, and are a goal worthy of the challenge they pose.

REFERENCES

Arnstein, S.R. 1969. A ladder of citizen participation. *Journal of the American Institute of Planners* 35(4): 216-224.

Canadian Universities Consortium Urban Environmental Management Training and Technology Transfer Program (CUC UEM TTTP). 1999. *Planning for Sustainable Tourism Development at the Local Level: A Workbook.* Bangkok, Thailand: Canadian International Development Agency.

Chartered Institute of Public Finance and Accountancy (CIPFA) (1995). *Corporate Governance: A Framework for Public Service Bodies.* London, UK: CIPFA.

Eber, S. (Ed). 1992. *Beyond the Green Horizon: Principles for Sustainable Tourism.* Godalming, UK: World Wide Fund for Nature.

Go, F. 1993. The role of socially responsible tourism management. In W. Nuryanti (Ed.), *Universal Tourism: Enriching or Degrading Culture? Proceedings of the International Conference on Cultural Tourism.* Yogyakarta, Indonesia: Gadjah Mada University Press.

Simmons, D. 1994. Community participation in tourism planning. *Tourism Management,* 15(2): 98-105.

World Tourism Organization. 1994. *National and Regional Tourism Planning: Methodologies and Case Studies.* New York: Routledge.

Chapter 9

Carrying Capacity As a Tool for Tourism Destination Management

Pallavi Mandke

INTRODUCTION

Tourism depends on the natural and human environment for its existence. To host large numbers of tourists and provide them with a satisfactory experience, destinations must cope with high demand and pressure on their infrastructure and basic services. High consumption of water and energy, the generation of waste, and the utilization of transportation infrastructure by tourists are matters of concern for managers at most destinations. As pointed out by Gunn (1994), this mounting pressure on environmental services results when planners do not plan adequately. After the Earth Summit in Rio de Janiero in 1992, all industries, including tourism, came under environmental scrutiny, bringing sustainable tourism—an approach that aims to destroy the boom and bust syndrome and manage resources sustainably—into focus. Several environmental management tools such as environmental management systems (EMS), environmental impact assessment (EIA), and cleaner production have been well received and widely implemented as tools that can help to achieve sustainable tourism. However, carrying capacity, another potentially potent tool of environmental management, is a concept that, due to its complexity, has not been widely accepted as a tool for sustainable tourism planning.

Community Destination Management in Developing Economies
© 2006 by The Haworth Press, Inc. All rights reserved.
doi:10.1300/5140_10

This chapter looks at carrying capacity as a tool to enrich the quality of visitor experience and the quality of life of the local community and to protect the environment by identifying and reducing negative visitor impacts. The chapter attempts to explain the concepts and issues of carrying capacity and to translate the concept into a practical management tool. It is directed at destination managers who are trying to reduce visitor impacts on a destination, and at an audience interested in further refining the use of carrying capacity in sustainable tourism and environmental management.

CONCEPTS AND ISSUES RELATED TO CARRYING CAPACITY IN TOURISM

The concept of carrying capacity was initiated by the development of a holistic definition of environment, including physical, cultural, social, economic, and political aspects, and of a better understanding of environmental sustainability for tourism. In the 1960s, looking at capacity and how it affects the future of a destination became a new approach to tourism planning in North America and parts of Europe. Since then, it has often faced criticism. Initially it set out to address the seemingly straightforward question, How much is too much? But predetermining visitor limits was not an easy task; attempts to answer the question at the heart of carrying capacity generated further questions, such as the following:

- How will this magic number be determined?
- Who will determine this number?
- What time factor should be considered while determining carrying capacity—a day, a year, or the life of the destination/attraction?
- How do we know that the relationship between the number of visitors and impacts is always inversely proportional? Impacts caused by many well-behaved visitors can be much less than those of a few ill-behaved visitors.
- Would the carrying capacity for a larger area be determined by the limit for the most sensitive parts of the area?
- How will carrying capacity be enforced?

Despite issues surrounding the discussion on carrying capacity, the concept received renewed attention because its complex and comprehensive exercise could lead to a better understanding of limits to acceptable change in an area. According to Glasson and colleagues (1995), the fundamental components of carrying capacity are quality of environment and visitor experience implying that carrying capacity is not merely a game of magic numbers but that it involves both quantitative and qualitative capacities of a destination.

Carrying capacity can be a management tool that, when used to identify limits to growth, can be the first step toward preventing negative visitor impacts and limiting the degree of change that can be safely accommodated without altering the special character of the tourist destination. The concept of carrying capacity, however, is difficult to define. The best definition is one provided by Glasson and colleagues (1995), describing carrying capacity as the "physical, biological, social and psychological capacity of the environment to support tourist activity without diminishing environmental quality or visitor satisfaction." It is also relative and specific to each destination, since the setting of limits depends on the desired condition and causes of impact at each destination. Setting out to identify universally applicable magic numbers or limits is therefore an unrealistic expectation.

CARRYING CAPACITY AS A TOOL
OF TOURISM MANAGEMENT

After one understands the issues that surround carrying capacity, the challenge that remains is to translate the concept into practical application. A number of elements of carrying capacity exist, which are essential to destination management.

Perspectives

To determine carrying capacity, destination planning authorities should first decide from whose perspective the exercise should be carried out: visitors, the local community, the environment, or the entire destination. The visitor's perspective will focus on the quality of experience, and will be short-term, limited to the number of hours or days spent by the visitor at the destination. The perspective of the community, the environment, and the site will be long term and will focus on the quality of life.

Carrying Capacity Dimensions

Some important dimensions of carrying capacity include the following:

- *Physical dimension.* Concerns physical space and infrastructure at a destination. Issues such as the quality and quantity of accommodations, transportation, water supply, and energy, deal with the impact of increasing numbers of visitors on the physical attributes of a destination. The physical dimension is easier to measure than other dimensions of carrying capacity.
- *Ecological dimension.* Focuses on the ability of the natural environment, such as flora, fauna, soil, air, water—both individually and as ecosystems—to cope with visitor impacts. The ecological dimension is difficult to measure and monitor but is of utmost importance, especially if the ecosystem is sensitive and involves endangered species.
- *Social dimension.* Deals with sociocultural aspects of tourism for which the number, activities, and demands of visitors affect the social fabric and cultural integrity of the community. Overcrowding and changes in social and cultural patterns are some examples of social carrying capacity.
- *Economic dimension.* Addresses the community's ability to cope with new and increasing economic activities related to tourism without marginalizing traditional economic activities of the community. This dimension is also concerned with the seasonality of tourism and its effects on the economy of the destination and labor force.
- *Political dimension.* Focuses on political will, organizational capacity, public and private cooperation, and public involvement in decision making.

Taking these dimensions into account, Glasson and colleagues (1995) have explained carrying capacity in a formula:

$$CC = f(Q,T,N,U,DM,AB)$$

where carrying capacity (CC) is the function (f) of the:

- *Quality* of resources available
- *Tolerance* of those resources to visitor use
- Actual *Number* of visitors at the site or setting
- Type of *Use* or visitor activity undertaken
- *Design* and *Management* of visitor facilities in the setting
- *Attitude* and *Behavior* of visitors on the site, and similarly of the site managers

The Time Factor

The time factor in carrying capacity changes depending on whose perspective is being considered. From the visitor's perspective, in which the quality of experience is the focus, the carrying capacity should be determined for the duration of a visitor's stay (e.g., half a day). On the other hand, from the community's or the site's perspective, in which quality of life is the focus, the carrying capacity should be determined for the long term (e.g., the life of the community or the site, appropriately divided over a day or year).

IMPLEMENTING CARRYING CAPACITIES

In order to clearly determine carrying capacities, the potential impacts should first be identified, after which indicators can be developed to monitor these impacts. Since many destinations and tourism sites are government properties, it is up to local authorities to operate within the determined carrying capacities. Wherever the site or facility management and operation responsibilities are shared by the private sector, it becomes important for the private sector to operate within limits and with the government in the role of "watchdog" to enforce implementation. In addition to regulations, economic incentives and awards for voluntary compliance can be applied.

MONITORING INDICATORS

Monitoring indicators help determine if a destination is operating within its carrying capacities. These indicators should reflect the desired conditions of the destination and should identify impacts that create undesirable changes. Not all concerns identified in the impact list prepared by the destination managers need to be monitored or can generate practical indicators.

Some broad quantitative indicators of determining capacities include the following:

- *Volume.* Peak, hourly, daily, weekly, or yearly volumes of various types of visitors (e.g., bed nights, visits, or visitor days)
- *Density.* Number of persons per hectare or square foot for different activities and for different locations
- *Market mix.* Number of visitor units relative to resident units
- *Time.* Amount of time spent by a visitor at the destination

Qualitative indicators of carrying capacity can be, for instance, the satisfaction level of visitors and the satisfaction level of residents as well as the time taken to access services, attractions, etc.

CONCLUSION

Carrying capacity is a well-recognized tool, but little documentation is available concerning how it should be implemented and what the effects have been in places where it has been implemented. This chapter attempts to provide guidelines on how to determine carrying capacities for a destination, for which carrying capacities are not necessarily numbers but can also be determined by specifying the quality of usage.

REFERENCES

Glasson, J., Godfrey, K., Goodey, B., Absalom, H., and Borg, J.V.D. (1995). *Toward visitor impact management: Visitor impacts, carrying capacity and management responses in Europe's historic towns and cities.* Aldershot, UK: Ashgate.
Gunn, Clare A. (1994). *Tourism planning: Basics, concepts, cases,* Third edition. Washington, DC: Taylor & Francis.

Chapter 10

Singapore's "Tourism Unlimited" and Transport Infrastructure Management

Anthony T. H. Chin

INTRODUCTION

Singapore is recognized as one of the leading tourism destinations in the world, and is presented here as an example of successful destination management. Particular circumstances affect the success of the destination, but all destinations can learn from its integrated approach and high-quality infrastructure and service. One of the important dimensions of the success is the commitment of government to tourism and to a planning and implementation process.

Singapore's tourism blueprint for the new millennium, "Tourism Unlimited," set out two objectives: first, to bring the world to Singapore through the enhancement of Singapore's own attractiveness as a must-see destination, and second, to bring Singapore to the world through Singapore's active participation in the development of the region's tourism through win-win partnerships that will lead to the creation of new tourism space outside Singapore. This is a logical approach, given the proximity of Singapore to the rest of Southeast Asia (see Table 10.1). The achievement of these goals requires the uninhibited movement of tourism, appropriate infrastructure, and political and economic stability that will lead to cooperation between governments through bold and enabling legislation.

Community Destination Management in Developing Economies
© 2006 by The Haworth Press, Inc. All rights reserved.
doi:10.1300/5140_11

TABLE 10.1. Air distances (km) between selected Asian cities.

City	BKK	HK	KL	MNL	SIN	JKT	HCM	BSB
BKK	****	1719	1203	2199	1443	2324	745	1859
HK	1719	****	2530	1125	2576	3265	1513	1939
KL	1203	2530	****	2480	334	1173	1022	1496
MNL	2199	1125	2480	****	2373	2786	1601	1260
SIN	1443	2576	334	2373	****	883	1094	1278
JKT	2324	3265	1173	2786	883	****	1902	1533
HCM	745	1513	1022	1601	1094	1902	****	1120
BSB	1859	1939	1496	1260	1278	1533	1120	****

BKK: Bangkok
HK: Hong Kong
KL: Kuala Lumpur
MNL: Manila
SIN: Singapore
JKT: Jakarta
HCM: Ho Chi Minh City
BSB: Brisbane

Tourism arrivals for 2004 were 8,328,118, which represents and increase of 35 percent from 2003 (Singapore Tourism Board, 2005). In 2004, Singapore's main source market was Asia with 6,078,757 international arrivals. Indonesia was by the biggest market with 1,765,321 visitors. Visitors from China totaled 880,188, and 537,254 people visited from Malaysia. Singapore attracted 1,070,734 visitors from Europe, with the United Kingdom accounting for 457,238 of those arrivals, and 333,117 tourists from the United States. Total expenditures of visitors on a yearly basis in 2004 were 5,425,000,000 Singapore dollars, up from 4,315,200,200 Singapore dollars in 2003 (Singapore Tourism Board, 2005b). Regional links will not only prolong the average length of stay but will also, through bilateral tourism pacts, contribute to Association of Southeast Asian Nations (ASEAN) tourism initiatives and ensure unity in the region's destination marketing.

One of the key initiatives for 2001 was the introduction of the Singapore Tourism Specialist Program. Its objective was to develop top travel agencies as Singapore specialists. The program, launched at the ASEAN Tourism Forum, took off across Southeast Asia for the rest of the year. In this first phase, Singapore Tourism Board (STB) targeted 300 travel agents, who were invited to attend a special training program to equip them with the latest destination information on Singapore. The second phase revolved around staging international events to ensure a year-round agenda of high-profile happenings that would project the island as a world-class event destination. These events were encapsulated in STB's marketing campaign, which aimed at a concerted worldwide effort to emphasize Singapore's image transformation. This campaign focused on Singapore's diverse products and lifestyles, the multiethnic tapestry, and the successful ultramodern commercial New Asia–Singapore hub.

The success of this strategy hinged upon several factors. First, the packaging of Singapore as a tourist destination hub to the region required close regional cooperation. Second, ease and convenience of travel to the island would be greatly enhanced by a more liberal transport environment within Asia. Third, the availability and constant upgrading of transport infrastructure such as ports, airports, and efficient land transport network would enable congestion-free travel.

TRANSPORT INFRASTRUCTURE DEVELOPMENT

It must be noted that investment in transport infrastructure was not made primarily for the tourism sector but rather to facilitate economic development and growth. Priority was given to develop the island into an entrepôt hub, taking advantage of its unique and advantageous location within Southeast Asia. Today the Port of Singapore is the world's busiest port, and Changi International Airport (CIA) has been rated among the world's best by many travelers. However, in recent years, multimodal transport has assumed greater importance, with a resurgence in the cruise industry and the development of Singapore into a tourism hub. The government has embarked on a concerted effort to provide complementary infrastructure support for fly/cruise and cruise/fly packages.

Singapore Cruise Center

A sum of 50 million Singapore dollars was allocated to develop and promote Singapore as the cruise gateway to the Asia-Pacific. The infrastructure support is in the form of three terminals: the international passenger terminal (IPT), the regional ferry terminal (RFT), and the domestic ferry terminal (DFT), which cater to international, regional, and domestic seaborne travelers respectively. The Tanah Merah ferry terminal (TMFT) handles regional ferry services going mainly to Bintan in Indonesia and the east coast of Peninsular Malaysia. More than 50 exotic destinations and ports are close to Singapore; the region has more tropical islands and beaches than the Caribbean.

Air Transportation

In 2004, CIA handled a record high of 30 million passenger movements and 1.7 million tons of cargo. Terminals, programs, facilities, and services are constantly upgraded.

Capacity expansion far ahead of demand and anticipated economic recovery is the norm. For example, the 244.2 million U.S. dollar finger-pier extension of Terminal 1 was opened officially on January 22, 2000. The additional 14 new aerobridge gates bring the total number of aerobridge gates in Terminal 1 to 33. These new gates are designed to accommodate all types of commercial aircraft, including the latest extended Boeing 777-200. Some of the gates are configured for easy modifications, to accommodate larger future aircraft. A further 20 million U.S. dollars was spent on upgrading the departure and arrival halls of Terminal 1. CIA is in the middle of another expansion with the construction of a third terminal at a cost of 1.5 billion Singapore dollars. The projected opening of the new terminal is for 2008, and Terminal 3 will 28 more aerobridge gated to the airport, up to eight of which will have the ability to handle the newer generations of large aircraft. This will give the airport the capacity to manage 20 million passengers a year and bring its total capacity to 64 million until the year 2020. In addition, passengers will find making interterminal flight connections much easier after the opening of Terminal 3 with the installation of a new 135 million Singapore dollar automated people mover system being constructed by the Civil Aviation Authority of Singapore (CAAS) (Civil Aviation Authority of Singapore, 2005b).

In 2005, CIA won a total of 17 best airport awards and accolades from major international publications and organizations (Civil Aviation Authority of Singapore, 2005a).

Land Transportation

Since the mid-1970s, land transport strategies have focused on ensuring the smooth flow of passenger and freight traffic. Several instruments such as road pricing, a quota on automobile population, investments in public transport, and a comprehensive network of roads and other fiscal incentives and disincentives have been introduced to ensure that the agents of economic growth are mobile. The objective is to enhance the quality of life through efficient mobility.

The mission of the Land Transport Authority is to provide a quality, integrated, and efficient land transport system that meets the needs and expectations of Singaporeans, supports economic and environmental goals, and provides value for money. Improvements to the transport system must also be aimed at enhancing the quality of life for all Singaporeans. The objectives of a land transport policy include the following:

- Deliver a land transport network that is integrated, efficient, cost effective, and sustainable
- Plan, develop, and manage Singapore's land transport system to meet the nation's needs
- Optimize the use of our transport resources and safeguard the well-being of the traveling public
- Develop and implement policies to encourage commuters to choose the most appropriate mode of transport

Maintaining a Competitive Edge

The development of transportation infrastructure is just one important aspect of tourist sector enhancement. Simply putting an efficient transportation network into place does not attract tourists; one must take a holistic perspective of the industry.

The Tourism 21 Plan was launched in 1996. It is a strategic document that charts Singapore's path toward status as a tourism capital, taking into consideration the rapid changes brought about by technology and globalization, different demographics, and changing lifestyle patterns, needs, and preferences. The review recommended that the tourism industry focus on three broad strategic thrusts: the promotion of continual innovation in product development and marketing, the advancement of manpower as a key source of competitiveness, and a retooling of today's tourism business strategies.

Continual innovation in product development and marketing is one key area that can take advantage of advancements in information technology. A travel portal has been established to integrate industry members and enable online business-to-business and business-to-customer transactions.

A key element in the maintenance of competitiveness is the establishment of the Singapore Tourism Academy at Sentosa, a vertically integrated educational institution that provides all-around training in the industry and contributes to the transformation of Singapore into a regional tourism education hub. In addition, the Art of Service, a new nationwide campaign to introduce and develop the concept of service as a passionate performance, has been introduced. Several U.S. and U.K. universities are setting up hospitality and tourism programs in Singapore.

To help the industry adapt to the challenges of the new economy, the review recommended that the government adopt a more liberal approach to regulation and licensing. Other recommendations included promoting Singapore as a hub for tourism consultancy and research, encouraging professional and industry associations to base themselves in Singapore so as to develop a critical mass of business meetings and events, and grooming regional tour operators to enhance Singapore's external tourism initiatives. Customized or niche tourism experiences can be developed through differentiated and focused segment marketing such as cruise packages for seniors and spa and wellness programs. Major sports and arts events can be held in Singapore. New ways of cultivating event management competencies and a sponsorship culture are being explored to attract international events.

It is also apparent that the government must play an important role in the development of the tourist sector in Singapore. In developed economies, the spirit of innovation and creativity is supported by the stability that a matured market mechanism and institutions can offer, but most developing economies do not have that luxury. Market institutions are often not well developed, and economies are often ravaged by the inefficiencies of corruption, nepotism, the absence of well-defined laws and regulations, and the lack of an efficient regulatory framework and civil service to ensure that the system works. The issue of governance is often missing from the equation and, if left to the private sector, the development of the tourist sector will see—at best—pockets of success. Figure 10.1 summarizes the hypothesis that the government plays an essential role in the promotion of a holistic approach to the development of the tourist sector and in ensuring that the appropriate infrastructures are in place.

Finally, sustainability is possible only if a strong and growing economy is able to fuel proactive infrastructure investments in all sectors: air, sea, and land. To ensure and enhance mobility for tourists, effective land traffic management schemes must be in place to complement infrastructure development. Travel modes must be efficiently integrated to minimize travel time between transfers. The presence of good government and an efficient and a proactive civil service will support an open, competitive business environment. From a macro perspective, the presence of strong and competitive

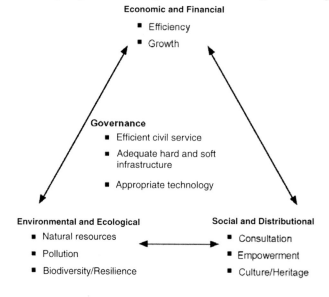

FIGURE 10.1. Governance, sustainable transportation infrastructure development, and the tourist sector.

modes, such as an airline able to network benefits and economies and form alliances and partnerships, are vital to bringing tourists to Singapore. Furthermore, the liberalization of the air sector would bring in tremendous multiplier benefits to the region.

CONCLUSION

Singapore is recognized as one of the leading metropolitan areas in Asia with high-quality public transportation, clear air, a rule of law, and now a government commitment to support tourism as well as other areas of economic activity. The country's high-quality infrastructure serves as an excellent backdrop to exploiting the destination's unique culture as well as its attractions. Approval of two integrated resorts with casinos will further add to the destination's appeal.

The country's marketing strategy with its new Uniquely Singapore brand was successfully launched in Singapore in March 2004, followed by a launch in Berlin at the ITB (Internationale Tourismus-Börse/International Tourism Stock Exchange) trade show and in various key markets. Uniquely Singapore has been well received globally, evident from the steady increase in brand awareness and recall among identified target segments.

It is interesting to note that the Singapore Tourism Board has created two divisions: the Resource Development Division and the Travel and Hospitality Business Division. The Resource Development Division supports the growth of tourism by doing the following:

- Formulating strategies and implementing plans to develop the capability, quality and quantity of tourism manpower
- Driving and/or facilitating the development of "hard" and "soft" infrastructure to support the strategic tourism units and tourism growth. Hard infrastructure refers to land issues while soft infrastructure pertains to visa issues.
- Guiding and/or facilitating the creation of an enabling, pro-enterprise legislative framework for the tourism sector
- Promoting the development and adoption of technologies that will enhance the competitiveness of the tourism industry and tourism partners (Singapore Tourism Board, 2005a)

The Travel and Hospitality Business Division is involved in creating marketing initiatives for hospitality and travel services, in investment promotion, and in industry development. This division works with strategic tourism units to meet the accommodation needs of target markets. Creating *marketing initiatives* involves promoting concepts and products that reveal Singapore's appeal as an attractive destination to potential tourists. *Investment promotion* involves discovering and implementing new, exciting foreign concepts, and *industry development* focuses on establishing sustainable growth, well-being, and vibrancy in the public and private sectors (Singapore Tourism Board, 2005a).

Although it is impossible to duplicate the experience, a number of lessons can be learned from this destination's integrated approach to economic development using tourism as a major tool in creating more opportunities and revenues for Singapore.

REFERENCES

Civil Aviation Authority of Singapore (2005a). Singapore Changi Airport bags five more awards. Press releases, October 24. Available online at: http://www.changi. airport.com.sg/changi/press_release_content.jsp?DYNAMIC_FOLDER%3C% Efolder_id=9853823208128582&CONTENT%3C%3Ecnt_id=101352981848 39522&FOLDER%3C%3Efolder_id=2534374302024632&ASSORTMENT% 3C%3East_id=1408474395181068&bmUID=1131631929559.

Civil Aviation Authority of Singapore (2005b). Terminal 3 development. Available online at: http://www.changi.airport.com.sg/changi/level3.jsp?FOLDER%3C% 3Efolder_id=2534374302023762&ASSORTMENT%3C%3East_id=1408474 395181062.

Singapore Tourism Board (2005a). Overview. Available online at: http://app.stb. com.sg/asp/ind/ind.asp.

Singapore Tourism Board (2005b). Research and statistical information. Available online at: http://app.stb.com.sg/asp/tou/tou02.asp.

Chapter 11

Urban Environmental Tourism Destination Management: Phimai Case Study, Nakhon Ratchasima Province, Thailand

Pawinee Sunalai

INTRODUCTION

Phimai, an urban heritage area, is located about 300 kilometers from Bangkok in Northeast Thailand's Nakhon Ratchasima province. Historically, Phimai was a trade center and an important gateway from the Moon River basin to Cambodia and to towns in the Chao Phraya River basin. It was part of the Khmer Empire for several centuries. Presently, Phimai is seen as both a tourist destination and an important model of economic development. However, visitor experiences, interpretation of resources, and tourist impact on heritage resources are still the important issues for Phimai with respect to sustainable development.

This paper is intended to present some techniques for physical environmental management that have been recommended for implementation in Phimai town, and to explore issues related to these suggestions. It focuses on the improvement of the interpretive programs of two main tourist attractions in Nakhon Ratchasima province, Phimai Historic Park (which contains the largest Khmer stone sanctuary in Thailand, built in the style of Angkor Wat) and Phimai National Museum, to enhance tourist appreciation of the sites and increase both length of tourist stay and amount of spending in Phimai.

Community Destination Management in Developing Economies
© 2006 by The Haworth Press, Inc. All rights reserved.
doi:10.1300/5140_12

TOURISM SITUATION OF PHIMAI

Although Phimai's primary occupation is agriculture, tourism is now becoming an important additional source of income. Out of Phimai's several tourist attractions, tourists visit two places most often: Phimai Historical Park and Phimai National Museum. Each year, approximately 350,000 people visit Phimai Historical Park, whereas the museum receives only 35,000 visitors per year. Previously, boundaries and zoning guidelines for the historic area of Phimai were not clearly defined, and enforcement of building restrictions was weak. Consequently, many buildings were constructed without proper control by those seeking business opportunities in the historic site area. Building design and color have also had a visual impact on historical resources in Phimai.

Most tourists are domestic visitors. Typically, they visit only the park and the museum and do not spend time within the city. Consequently, they do not leave with a sense of the historic character of Phimai. At the same time, the community does not benefit from this tourism as it should. In order to increase tourists' length of stay in Phimai, consideration should be given to making the physical environment of Phimai more attractive and more interesting. Phimai town and the historic sites would then generate more income (see Figure 11.1).

FIGURE 11.1. Map of attractions in Phimai.

MANAGEMENT ISSUES FOR PHIMAI CITY

In terms of providing infrastructure and facilities, the local government of Phimai municipality is responsible for Phimai city. They do not manage the historical sites, which are the responsibility of Thailand's Fine Arts Department. The following is an enumeration of issues to be addressed in Phimai.

Parking and Movement of Tourists and Traffic

The parking area for Phimai Historical Park is currently located in front of the sanctuary, creating traffic and air pollution in the area.

Along the Chomsudasaded Road, no sidewalk for pedestrian traffic is available due to the intrusion of commercial enterprises, residences, and bus terminals on both sides of the street. Consequently tourists are forced to walk on the street, which is inconvenient and unsafe (see Photo 11.1).

Green Area/Shading for Tourists

Only a few trees shade the road on which tourists walk. At noontime, when the heat is most oppressive, the lack of shade can create considerable discomfort.

PHOTO 11.1. Lack of pathway for tourists.

Urban Development

Most new buildings were constructed without design controls. The traditional wood houses and shops that gave the town its unique historical character are gradually disappearing as a result of this new development. Large buildings now overshadow the sanctuary site (see Photo 11.2).

Although building restrictions are now in place, they are not effectively enforced. These factors combine to produce a negative visual impact that affects the skyline around the sanctuary. In addition, the colors, sizes, types, and materials of nearby advertising signage also affect the serenity of the sanctuary and the surrounding area (see Photo 11.3).

Shopping Area

Most stores in the Phimai area sell everyday items used by the residents of Phimai city. Very few provide items that tourists might be interested in buying, such as clothes, postcards, or cast reproductions of carvings.

PHOTO 11.2. Conflicts between the development of the surrounding area and a historic site.

PHOTO 11.3. Visual effects of signage on the historic site without effective control.

Other Environmental Issues

The increasing number of visitors has created problems with sewage and litter disposal. Without public sewage treatment for Phimai city, large quantities of residential wastewater are released directly into the Moon River, deteriorating its water quality. Flooding is also a problem for Phimai, which can deter tourists from visiting the town.

SUGGESTED STRATEGIES TO IMPROVE PHIMAI'S URBAN ENVIRONMENT

Redirecting Tourist Traffic via Victory Gate

Restructuring the pattern of visitation so that tourists enter the town through the historic Victory Gate entrance would promote the sanctuary in its larger context from the moment they enter Phimai (see Figure 11.2). By walking along Chomsudasaded Road to the sanctuary, visitors would develop a feeling for the community's living heritage before reaching the sanctuary and would better appreciate the size of the area inside the ancient walls. Interpretive panels for

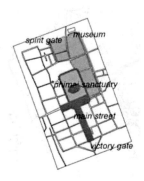

FIGURE 11.2. Map of Phimai area.

Phimai Main Street could feature text and drawings about the historic and contemporary significance of sites along the way (see Photo 11.4 and Figure 11.3).

The following are some recommendations for the development of Chomsudasaded Road, which address the aforementioned problems of Phimai's physical environment. However, it must also be stressed that opinions from local people and relevant agencies are necessary to the decision-making process.

- Explore the possibility of relocating bus stops outside Victory Gate. Relocating bus terminals would reduce traffic, air pollution, and safety issues for tourists. Since this change would affect locals, public hearings must be held to evaluate the feasibility and impact of this change. If this change is feasible, tourist services and facilities such as parking lots, public toilets, souvenir shops, and food stores should be provided as well.
- Explore the possibility of a restricted parking lot in front of the sanctuary, for use by officials only. To encourage tourists to enter Phimai town through Victory Gate, tourists could be dropped off in front of the sanctuary.
- Improve sidewalk access, plant trees, and increase the amount of green space. This would provide attractive landscaping and shade to Phimai town.

- Relocate unattractive overhead electricity and communications wires underground. This would be beneficial in the long term, but implementation will be expensive, and will require a high level of cooperation between various government agencies.

PHOTO 11.4. View of the Phimai Sanctuary from Victory Gate.

FIGURE 11.3. Example of interpretive signage for Phimai's Main Street.

Linkage Between the Museum and Sanctuary

Currently, the location of the museum and the lack of effective signage and publicity at the sanctuary make it an underutilized resource. The museum and the sanctuary are often seen as separate attractions that are distant from each other. Most visitors drive between the two, increasing traffic congestion on roads even though the driving distance is actually much longer than the walking path from the sanctuary's outer northern gate to the museum. Linkages would physically connect the site and museum, and would help visitors see the two sites as one attraction. Improved physical linkages and signage would utilize the potential of the museum, increase visitation, give visitors a more complete picture of Phimai's history, and encourage tourists to stay longer (see Figure 11.4).

If the two sites were linked, a single-ticket fee structure for both the sanctuary and the museum could be introduced. This would attract more tourists and increase revenue to the museum. The tickets could be sold at both sites.

Alternative Walking Circuits

The proposed walkway options linking the museum and the sanctuary are presented in the following list. Five possible walking routes are available between the museum and sanctuary, based on two

FIGURE 11.4. Current (a) and potential (b) views along Anunthachinda Road from the junction with Chomsudasaded Road.

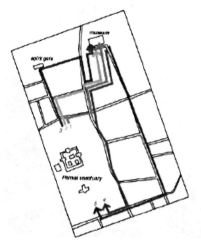

FIGURE 11.5. Suggested routes to link the museum and the sanctuary.

movement patterns for improved linkage (see Figure 11.5). Proper direction maps and signage for tourists along those routes would have to be provided at both the northern and southern outer gates.

> *Option 1.* Tourists start walking at Victory Gate, proceed through the sanctuary and outer northern sanctuary gate, and end at the museum.
>
> *Option 2.* Tourists start with a visit to the museum and then walk to the sanctuary (see Figure 11.6).

MANAGEMENT ISSUES
FOR PHIMAI HISTORICAL PARK

Interpretation of Phimai Historical Park

Currently, the sanctuary's history is presented in photographs, leaflets, books, models, and briefing notes for artifacts, historic gates, and ponds. These are economical ways to tell the story of the sanctuary, but they do not fully educate people about the significance of the site. Interpretive signage in the sanctuary should bring the carvings and buildings to life. These signs should present the information in a

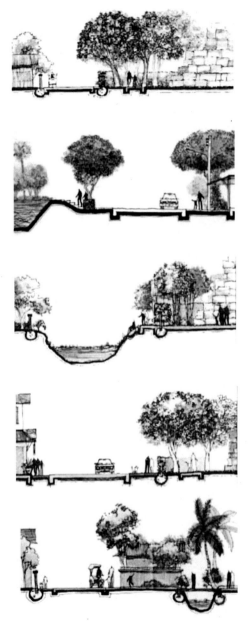

FIGURE 11.6. The proposed walking routes to link the museum and the sanctuary (a-e).

relevant and physically attractive way, without interfering with the site's visual integrity.

At the encouragement of the Department of Fine Arts, the Canadian Universities Consortium Urban Environmental Management (CUC UEM) Project has developed a video using virtual reality technology. An important element of a good interpretive program is to explore a site's history in an exciting way (see Photo 11.5 and Figure 11.7). This video, which tells the story of Phimai sanctuary, enables a visitor to develop a better appreciation of the heritage resource by digitally reconstructing the way the site must have looked a thousand years ago.

PHOTO 11.5. Phimai Sanctuary today.

FIGURE 11.7. Phimai Sanctuary fifty years ago (a) and 1,000 years ago (b).

Tourism Impacts on Sanctuary

350,000 visitors per year can negatively impact the sanctuary's physical condition. In addition, the annual three-day light-and-sound performance held at the site, accommodating 1,000 to 2,000 visitors, plus smaller light-and-sound performances once or twice a month, also affect the site. Carrying capacity is a significant issue here. The responsible authorities must monitor it at the site and then design appropriate mitigative measures.

MANAGEMENT ISSUES FOR PHIMAI NATIONAL MUSEUM

The Phimai National Museum attracts around 35,000 visitors annually, or 10 percent of the tourists who visit Phimai sanctuary. This low visitation rate is due to the museum's location (behind and out of sight of the main sanctuary), poor directional signage, uncomfortable indoor temperatures in the spring, and unattractive interpretation (see Photo 11.6).

At present, the layout of artifacts within the museum does not take sufficient advantage of the available historical resources. Little or no interpretation draws visitors into the exhibits and artifacts. In

PHOTO 11.6. Phimai Museum.

many instances, the displays fail to generate adequate interest. In order to increase the number of visitors to the museum, the interpretation, accessibility, and comfort of the museum need to be improved.

Interpretation of the Phimai National Museum

Displays need to be redesigned in light of an overall theme or story. At present, the displays appear lifeless and dull, and unrelated to one another. To encourage the use of the museum as a source of interesting and relevant information about Phimai's history, the following changes to the layout and the use of artifacts in the museum are recommended.

- Good-quality artifacts that are strong representative samples of the museum collection should be located in the museum's entrance hall. This will improve visual interest in the museum and draw visitors to the displays.
- The displays could be organized to create a journey though the museum, taking visitors from a general history to specific aspects of Phimai. Placing the video of images of the Phimai sanctuary at the end of the museum route would work well. This would help create an exploration of the dual themes of the general history of Khmer architecture and civilization in Thailand, and the specific history and artifacts of Phimai.
- More interpretive information on the symbolism, structure, and other interesting aspects of the artifacts could be provided. This would help tourists understand the significance of many of the objects in the museum.

Phimai Museum Adaptations

During the hot spring months, temperatures in the museum can become unbearable. The costs of installation and maintenance of air conditioning in the museum are currently not affordable; a low-technology solution, based on cooling techniques found in traditional Thai architecture, should be explored. A wide range of techniques for ventilation systems to deal with this issue include the following:

- The installation of several ceiling fans would draw warm air toward the ceiling.

- A number of openings around the lower part of the building, close to ground level, could be installed to bring cool air into the building.
- To further cool the incoming air, gardens could be planted at these points. Drawing the air though vegetation can lower the temperature by several degrees.

Access Improvements

The historical interpretive experience of the museum site could be enhanced along the sidewalk. The placement of some artifacts in this area, along with brief interpretive details, would begin to develop the story of the Khmer architecture and artifacts of Thailand even before visitors reached the museum.

CONCLUSION

In addition to the sanctuary and museum, Phimai has other potential historic attractions. The community should be presented as a historic town, not just as a place with selected tourist assets. A piecemeal approach to tourism and urban environmental problems is not adequate to solve Phimai's problems. These urban environmental management factors need to be addressed in the broader context of tourism, and the physical and social climate in which they are situated. A balance between concerns for economic development, environmental conditions, and cultural heritage preservation for Phimai is essential. The development of a more sustainable tourism industry will benefit not only individual businesses and historic sites, but can also help to improve Phimai for all its residents. More effective coordination between government agencies and public consultation will be necessary to enact many of these recommendations. However, these suggestions should not be considered final solutions; they have been designed to provoke the debate and further input that will be necessary to produce a community action plan. Involvement from stakeholders and relevant government agencies must be a major component of any such planning process. Phimai city's biggest challenge will be the coordination of responsibilities for different actors and agencies.

Chapter 12

Managing Urban Heritage Resources Within a Cultural Tourism Context

Walter Jamieson

INTRODUCTION

For any tourism destination, local heritage resources are among the major visitor attractions. Many urban destinations understand the importance of heritage resources for tourism development and are seeking ways to maintain and protect them while dealing with the many issues facing urban administrations. It is difficult to allocate scarce financial resources to the restoration and rehabilitation of heritage buildings, especially when city residents face a number of other urgent problems, such as access to clean water, reliable solid waste management, and low-cost public transportation. The chapter on destination management discusses these issues in detail.

The preservation of heritage is a luxury many developing countries are simply unable to afford. Administrators must maintain and enhance their heritage resources within a legislative and political environment that, in most cases, places low priority on heritage preservation. This is clearly a political issue to be resolved at the local level, but sufficient evidence supports the argument that investment in heritage resources can produce economic development if the heritage resource process is properly managed and marketed. This chapter takes the position that support exists at the local level for the protection of resources through both public investment and regulatory control.

Community Destination Management in Developing Economies
© 2006 by The Haworth Press, Inc. All rights reserved.
doi:10.1300/5140_13

In an era of economic restraint and increased competition, growing pressure to manage heritage attractions by balancing the needs of the visitor, the protection of a city's heritage, and the daily needs of its residents is occurring. This is a complex process, involving development of comprehensive management plans to combine the preservation of cultural heritage with economic development. Since tourism development is in part a business activity, any solution must be effective in an environment in which competition for tourists and resources comes from many sources.

Whether a site is a single building or a complex cultural landscape, appropriate techniques must be developed to handle such diverse issues as determination of visitor behavior and motivation, assessment of site and destination characteristics, and comprehension and implementation of carrying capacity strategies. This chapter provides only an overview of some strategies and techniques involved in heritage preservation and site management in urban areas.

To be successful, the management of heritage resources and sites— especially in an urban setting—must be a multidisciplinary activity. It must involve traditional heritage preservation in the areas of conservation, curatorship, design, interpretation, research, building rehabilitation, and the protection and enhancement of crafts. It also requires an understanding of such diverse fields as urban planning, architecture, real estate finance, building of partnerships, public participation, and product development. The process works successfully only when the concerns of all disciplines and perspectives are represented.

HERITAGE RESOURCE MANAGEMENT ISSUES

Preservation Philosophy

The central issue in heritage site management, whether addressing the management of a single building or an entire protected area, is how best to protect heritage resources and values. This decision is influenced by finances, the skill level of stakeholders, the commitment of key decision makers to quality preservation, the need for heritage environments to support modern-day activities, and the wear and tear associated with daily urban life.

A number of international charters are available to help municipal administrations develop standards and approaches to ensure that the community is developing its heritage resources in ways that meet the needs of the cultural tourism market. Some of the pertinent charters include the following:

- The International Council on Monuments and Sites (ICOMOS) Venice Charter (in cases of building preservation, this charter is seen as the basis for the protection of resources)
- The ICOMOS Cultural Tourism Charter
- The ICOMOS Charter for the Conservation of Historic Towns and Urban Areas

On a regular basis, heritage management professionals struggle with many issues: what level of restoration is appropriate, what constitutes sympathetic rehabilitation, how to ensure authenticity, how to reconcile the use of traditional versus modern materials, what methods exist for preserving traditional ways of life and values, and how to determine what levels of change are appropriate, given the nature of a city's heritage. Every country has professionals who are able to address these philosophical issues and have a significant effect on the quality of the area's resource management. It should be stressed that the answers to these important questions form the basis for ongoing management of heritage resources.

No right or wrong answers exist for heritage resource management. The challenge is to achieve a balance between meeting the needs of good-quality heritage resource management and providing residents with economic development opportunities.

Changing Visitor Tastes and Expectations

Within the context of tourism, heritage resources are seen as attractions. Urban and site managers need to understand visitors' motivations and expectations in order to maintain the viability of heritage resources. They must have a good grasp of market research and promotion, know how to maintain a database of tourism trends, and make sure that a resource has the ability to meet visitor expectations.

Impacts of Visitors on Sites and the Larger Community

Some physical impacts on a resource can be easily dealt with through maintenance during the course of normal operation. Others can affect the long-term physical environment in a way that cannot be repaired. Constant monitoring must be implemented to ensure that visitors are not destroying the resource that is the very basis of the community's attractiveness to tourists. It is equally important to monitor and assess the social and cultural impact of tourism on residents of a community and their way of life.

Financing and Partnerships

In the past, the financing of heritage management work was seen largely as the responsibility of the public sector. Current practice clearly demonstrates that funding comes from not one, but many sources. Governments are still an important source of money, but the private sector and nongovernmental organizations are now seen as important partners. In addition, heritage resources should contribute to the financial life of the community. Income generated directly from attractions can have a positive impact on the larger community environment. The challenge is to monitor and report these economic impacts to the appropriate decision makers.

In all areas of development, partnerships are vital to the success of any initiative. Public and private partnerships can bring together different ideas, points of view, and contributions (financial, social, or political) that can combine to create a successful heritage strategy. The success level of a heritage initiative depends on how involved interest groups are in problem identification, action planning, design, and implementation. It is essential for any heritage site management strategy to bring together a common vision for the resource itself and for the larger environment in which it is located—and partnerships help to create this common vision.

Carrying Capacities and Limits of Growth

As has been observed in Chapter 9, carrying capacity measures the level of sustainable use. The issue is complex, particularly when a range of valued products and services must come from the same environment (as in the case of tourism). However, the question remains: How many tourists/visitors can be accommodated without threatening a resource's long-term viability?

The concept of carrying capacity has value when it draws attention to limits and thresholds. However, when dealing with real situations, the following factors must be considered:

- Tourism depends on attributes of the environment: its aesthetic qualities, maintenance of its social systems, and its ability to support active uses. Each attribute has its own response to different levels of use.
- The impact of human activity on a system may be gradual and may affect different parts of the system at different rates. Some environmental functions may be highly sensitive to human impact, whereas others degrade gradually in response to different levels of use.
- Every environment serves multiple purposes, and its sensitivity to different levels of use depends on the values of all users.

Different types of use have different impacts. Tourism managers need some form of measurement to reduce the risk that they will unknowingly step over biological or cultural thresholds that degrade the product, cause other adverse effects, or discourage customers.

Ways to measure carrying capacity include the following:

- *Tangible resource limits.* Limits are grouped into three classes: obstacles that can be overcome, obstacles that cannot reasonably be overcome because of current or anticipated financial and technological inputs, and resources that could be destroyed or fully consumed unless effective controls are applied.
- *Tolerance by the host population.* Outright hostility toward visitors can ruin visitors' experience and discourage new tourists.
- *Visitor satisfaction.* If visitors have negative experiences and attitudes, it can restrict the growth of tourism or cause a decline in the popularity of a destination area. One approach is to monitor the approval rating of departing visitors and, at the same time, assess perceptions and preferences in target populations of potential visitors. This marketing approach can reveal perceptual obstacles and tangible problems that lead to dissatisfaction but that can be removed by promoting the destination area.
- *Rates of growth or change.* Understanding the impact of rate of growth is important in measuring the carrying capacity of a site.

- *Indicators.* Understanding the previous measures is essential to determining whether a resource is beyond its carrying capacity, such as how well a site is absorbing visitor flows.

Carrying capacity management strategies consist of a set of either supply-side measures, which increase the availability of tourism services or increase the degree of utilization of a resource, or demand-side measures, which limit the use of a resource for tourism purposes. A distinction between hard and soft interventions can also be made; hard measures affect quantities or visitor numbers by rationing demand, cutting supply, or raising prices. Soft measures affect the behavior of the visitor or the entrepreneur.

THE NATURE AND PURPOSE OF URBAN DISTRICTS/COMMUNITY HERITAGE SITES

Although a city may view individual buildings as heritage resources, from a cultural tourism point of view, whole heritage districts and larger cultural landscapes tend to be more attractive. Urban and community heritage resources are complex and require a range of stakeholders to protect their value. Unlike single building or museum heritage sites, larger sites are dynamic and involve multiple decision makers and jurisdictions.

Successful site management requires an understanding of a range of community forces: global competition, declining resources for preservation, higher levels of competitiveness with other heritage areas and attractions, and the impact of demographic trends. In some cases, site management includes dealing with rapid technological and social change and turbulence as well as uncertainty in planning and management.

Urban heritage districts and sites can take many forms. It is important for urban destinations to think about the full range of resources and tourism potential that exists within their jurisdiction. The following list gives an indication of the richness of attractions that can be developed within many urban areas:

- Groups of buildings that physically and spatially comprise a historic or architectural theme

- Groups of buildings, structures, objects, and sites associated with particular ethnic, social, or economic groups
- Groups of buildings and structures that show industrial or technological developments
- Groups of buildings and structures that represent historical, commercial, political, and social development patterns
- Groups of sites, structures, and buildings that contain archaeological data
- Cultural landscapes
- Historic designated landscapes whose form, layout, or design—rather than events or persons—are the primary reason for protection
- Ethnographic landscapes characterized by the use of contemporary peoples, including hunting and gathering, religious or sacred ceremonies, and traditional meetings
- Corridors and linear resources—such as green belts, scenic roads, trails, rivers, and railway lines—that can be reached by car, foot, boat, horse, or rail. Given the number of jurisdictions they will cross, it is a challenge to resolve the planning, regulatory, and administrative issues for these resources, but they offer an opportunity to understand a living culture with a range of different spatial and geographical dimensions. They also offer chances for economic revitalization and interpretation.

Heritage areas contain a number of elements that must be understood and managed, including the following:

- *Ethnic tangible and intangible features.* Ethnic, minority, or religious groups, including settlement patterns, languages, lifestyles, values, housing types, work patterns, and schooling
- *Natural features.* Atmospheric elements, dominant landforms (e.g., bluffs, gorges, mountains), landforms, topography, vegetation, or water features (e.g., falls, pools, rapids, rivers, shorelines)
- *Sequences.* A sense of entry (e.g., gateways, visible approaches to dominant features or into districts), clarity of route, legibility of direction
- *Details and surfaces.* Street furniture, floorscape (e.g., pavement material and pattern)
- *Ambient qualities.* Climate, shadows, noise levels, smells, quality of light

- *Visible activities.* People observing people, everyday activities, special events
- *Intangibles.* Conversations, emotions, structure of society, values, ways of responding to change, the political decision-making structure, a sense of community

URBAN HERITAGE SITES
AND DISTRICT MANAGEMENT TECHNIQUES

Heritage areas are most often living and functioning communities, so the planning and management process must consider dimensions such as schools, recreation opportunities, air and water quality, transportation, housing costs, entertainment, job creation, participation opportunities, and the nature of the political system.

Some important techniques for ensuring that urban heritage site and resource developments achieve good quality are described in the following sections.

Government Programs

One task of the heritage site manager within urban areas is to narrow the wide range of available government programs to those that deal with a heritage district or area. Government intervention can include programs, subsidies, grants, technical assistance, and tax breaks and incentives.

Zoning

Zoning is often the most effective tool to maintain heritage. Because planning laws and regulations vary significantly, the site manager must understand the zoning process. Zoning techniques include heritage, large lot, overlay zoning, and cluster development options, and these must be understood by most urban planners at a destination.

Physical Planning Techniques

The "toolbox" of urban and physical planners contains a number of techniques to protect heritage resources, especially in a climate of change and under pressures incurred by high visitor numbers. These techniques include the following:

- Design and development controls
- Transfer of development rights to allow a landowner to sell or use the unused potential of his or her site in another location
- Preservation of views through zoning and urban design approaches
- Physical/land use planning to allow the site manager to anticipate such concerns as parking and transportation
- Employing land use legislation and techniques to protect heritage resources
- Easements, as legally enforceable instruments to transfer some rights of properties to other interests concerned with preservation and conservation. Easements can control the future of a property or piece of land and protect scenic corridors, open spaces, or the side of a building.
- Heritage area design guidelines and standards, which can guide changes in design plans for the addition of new buildings in historic environments. These guidelines are most effective when they are part of the zoning and planning regulatory process, and can be used to ensure that decisions are less arbitrary and subjective in nature. Design standards should respect these key elements: local styles and motifs, roof lines, the use of local building materials, environmental relationships, landscape design, height of buildings, setbacks of buildings from amenity features, the ratio of the building floor area to site area, coverage of the site by buildings and other structures, parking requirements, landscaping and open space, public access to amenity features, signs, and utility lines.

Urban Environmental Management Techniques

Urban heritage sites around the world are discovering that if they do not deal with the important issues of water, sewage, and transportation they will be unable to take advantage of their heritage environments. Visitors expect clean and safe environments. Managers should look for expertise and interest in their communities in the following spheres of concern: sustainable development, strategic planning, environmental impact assessment (EIA), auditing, economic instruments, ecosystem management, good governance, International Organization for Standardization (ISO) 14000 standards for quality management, integrated decision making, risk management, disaster preparedness, education, and training.

Interpretation

At tourist sites, little information is often made available about the site's significance, what to expect in terms of visitor behavior, and what the surrounding area offers in terms of visitor amenities. Telling the story of a community is an important tool for conservation, education, and economic development. Successful sites use interpretive techniques for various visitor segments; these can include guidebooks, maps, signage, a reception and visitor orientation center, a videotape presentation, movies, rental tape recorded tours, virtual reality presentations, recorded station stops, sound-and-light shows, festivals, reenactments, and guides and costumed interpreters working in the first or third person. This issue was discussed in detail in Chapter 6.

Visitor Management

A major task of urban heritage site management is dealing with visitor numbers, behavior, and impacts; limits exist on the use of any kind of site. Managers must ensure that visitor volumes do as little damage as possible to the site while guaranteeing its financial viability. Management strategies are available for dealing with visitor numbers, including restricting and limiting entry, reducing numbers of large groups, implementing a quota system, using pricing techniques to reduce demand, enforcing no-parking regulations, directing visitors to other sites, varying prices for select times of the week and year, taking reservations, using lotteries, extending hours, and limiting accommodations near the site.

Educating visitors helps reduce impacts on the site and culture. Techniques for visitor education can include interpreting and providing cultural values and guidelines; offering advice on accepting differences and adopting local customs; giving tips on proper behavior when photographing, purchasing goods, or tipping; setting expectations in advertising and promotional campaigns; providing literature and briefings on-site; and using interpreters and interpretive programs.

Visitor expectations can be better understood through visitor surveys and interviews, observation, videotape, public participation, photography, geographic information systems (GIS) via self-administered questionnaires, postal or administered surveys, and focus groups. Skilled surveyors should be employed to design and analyze results, and to deal with issues such as objectives, sample size, and bias.

Marketing

Market research and promotion are essential to ensure that the "right" kind of tourist will provide the maximum economic benefit to a site. These tools can also contribute to the maintenance of the full quality of the interpretive message and heritage resources.

Providing Visitor Amenities and Services

Making sure that visitors have a high-quality experience requires access to a range of visitor amenities and services. Some can be provided off-site, including hotels, guesthouses, hostels and campsites in varying price ranges, restaurants, and retail activities. Services such as car repair, grocery stores, e-mail connection, recreational facilities, entertainment possibilities, and health care should also be included in this list. Other services should be provided on-site, including access to clean drinking water, toilets, postal services, emergency medical services, garbage removal and disposal, and museum and heritage-site stores (the final two are important sources of income).

DEVELOPING A SITE MANAGEMENT PLAN

A management plan guides day-to-day operations and the ongoing physical and interpretive features of the site. Developing a plan can be difficult, because every plan needs to meet the requirements of several diverse stakeholders. The bottom line is that the site management plan must maintain and enhance heritage integrity and generate sufficient visitor volume to meet income requirements.

A plan is a living document that should be constantly updated to reflect ongoing changes in internal and external environments. Its objectives can include maintenance of the site's sense of place and integrity, preservation of the site's culturally significant dimensions, identification of issues of management concern, promotion of the roles of all stakeholders, and the creation of a management strategy to allow the site to meet a variety of challenges effectively.

The development of a good management strategy requires a process patterned on the following suggested series of steps:

1. *Getting started.* This involves determining the organizational approach, for instance, deciding who will lead the planning process and how differences of opinion and conflict will be handled; developing a realistic timeline; identifying the participants; and asking questions such as:
   * What are the current heritage conservation issues?
   * What is the level of community/group heritage awareness?
   * Has heritage site planning and management been successful in the past?
   * What are the priorities?
   * What are the strengths and weaknesses of the site?
   * What future opportunities and threats can the group/community foresee?

2. *Preparing a vision statement.* Determine the vision for the site's future by asking the following questions:
   * What is the identity of the heritage area/group?
   * How does the heritage area/site describe itself?
   * What are the issues facing the group?
   * How do these issues affect the development of a site's identity?
   * What does the site value and wish to retain?
   * Where are they now and where would they like to be in the future?

3. *Defining goals and objectives.* To achieve a vision statement, goals are required. Objectives—concrete activities that can be achieved within a specified period of time—can then be based on these goals. Progress toward objectives and goals should be monitored constantly.

4. *Defining problems.* Consultation with stakeholders can help determine problems and opportunities to be addressed in the management plan.

5. *Generating alternative plans and solutions.* Finding alternative strategies to solve problems can be a time-consuming process. It may require sophisticated cost-benefit analysis to make decisions on the best use of resources.

6. *Developing a management plan.* The plan must have these dimensions: decisions on specific actions, time periods, and priorities; a description of the implementation process; a projection of how the plan can be incorporated into the larger community and regional exercises; and budgets for site operations, staffing, volunteer management, and material supply. The plan must be realistic, and targets must be met within a reasonable time frame.

7. *Ongoing evaluation and monitoring.* Resources to monitor the success or failure of management strategies must be a priority.

ELEMENTS OF A HERITAGE SITE MANAGEMENT PLAN

Most heritage site management plans include the following factors:

- *Establishment of heritage significance.* Research into historical development, characteristics, cultural and religious significance, and authentic form should be a prerequisite.
- *Establishment of visitor carrying capacities.* If residents are living in the site area (e.g. urban historic districts), sociocultural and environmental impact analyses are important.
- *Conservation plans.* Conservation of the principal archaeological or historical features is a major consideration.
- *Visitor facilities and services.* The type and extent of visitor facilities and services are determined by projected visitor use. Facilities should be concentrated into one or a few areas and integrated into a visitor center complex, be located at or near the main entrance, and be accessible to visitors without impinging on the cultural feature. In historic districts, it is common to locate tourist facilities and related commercial enterprises in less important historic buildings whose interiors have been renovated and building facades preserved and restored. This can be

an interesting environment for tourists, and helps pay for building preservation.

- *Visitor-use plan.* The logical access and exit points and flow of visitors through the site are delineated. Direct access to fragile features may be prohibited, with a viewing area available and the number of visitors controlled at certain times to avoid excessive congestion or site deterioration. Signs and/or brochures can be used to explain site background and characteristics. Well-trained and (if necessary) multilingual guides should be available. Tourists should be informed of control measures, e.g., no littering or smoking.
- *Interpretation/presentation.* Presentations can include the use of live animations or technical means such as dioramas with mannequins and historical artifacts to explain, demonstrate, or re-create historical scenes and activities. Typical sounds and smells of the historical period or event can be reproduced, and visitor participation can be encouraged.
- *Monitoring.* Continuous monitoring of visitor satisfaction levels, sociocultural and environmental impacts on the facility, and visitor use should be conducted, and adjustments should be made where necessary.
- *Management of arts and handicraft activities.* These activities should be authentic, at least with respect to the use of local traditional skills, techniques, motifs, and materials. In some cases, minimum quality standards will be established for local handicrafts, which will then be inspected, approved, and—if the item meets the standard—identified with a stamp of certification. Arts and handicraft demonstrations can be interesting and educational for tourists, and may prompt them to make purchases.
- *Special cultural events.* Significant attractions for residents and tourists can include special cultural events—e.g., religious celebrations, art fairs, dance, music, drama, or general cultural festivals—and can also be an important way to revive and focus interest on the preservation of local cultural expressions that might otherwise be forgotten.
- *Admission pricing policies.* Admission fees can be charged at specific features, such as museums and zoos, to discourage casual visitors. Other techniques include offering reduced admission charges to residents.

CONCLUSION

Successful management of heritage resources and sites in the twenty-first century requires that certain conditions must be in place:

- Creative financing strategies
- A wide range of economic opportunities for all community residents
- Successful and professional marketing and promotion strategies
- Concern for the protection of heritage resources
- Managers who have high skill levels and can carry out a variety of multidisciplinary activities

The heritage management process is complex, involving a wide range of stakeholders. In addition to a knowledge of the commonly understood heritage resource management issues, urban heritage site management demands the consideration of many of the policy and operational issues dealt with by urban management in general. The objective is to ensure the preservation of the community's heritage and, at the same time, to meet the economic and social needs of residents. Achieving this balance is an important dimension of the "art" of managing urban heritage resources.

BIBLIOGRAPHY

Inskeep, E. 1991. *Tourism Planning: An Integrated and Sustainable Development Approach.* New York: Van Nostrand Reinhold.

Jamieson, W. 1991. The influence of international preservation charters in municipal planning and development control. Quebec: *Proceedings of the First International Symposium on World Heritage Towns.*

Jamieson, W. 1996. The planning and management of historic towns and areas in Canada. In *Monuments and Sites—Canada.* Sri Lanka: Sri Lanka National Committee of ICOMOS and the Central Cultural Fund of the Government of Sri Lanka and UNESCO for the International Council on Monuments and Sites (ICOMOS).

Jamieson, W. 1999. *Guidelines on Integrated Planning for Sustainable Tourism Development.* New York: United Nations Economic and Social Commission for Asia and the Pacific.

Jamieson, W., D. Getz, T. Jamal, and A. Noble. 2000. *Local Level Planning for Sustainable Tourism Development.* Canadian Universities Consortium Urban Environmental Management Project at the Asian Institute of Technology.

Jamieson, W. and P. Mandke. 2000a. The role of urban environmental management in resolving urban tourism destination management problems. In *Tourism—A Strategic Industry in Asia and Pacific: Defining Problems and Creating Solutions (Conference Proceedings).* Sydney: Asia Pacific Tourism Association.

Jamieson, W. and P. Mandke. 2000b. Urban tourism and environmental sustainability—Taking an integrated approach. In M. Robinson, R. Sharpley, N. Evans, P. Long, and Swarbrooke J. (Eds.), *Developments in Urban and Regional Tourism.* Sunderland: The Center for Travel and Tourism and Distance Education Publishers, Ltd.

Jamieson, W. and A. Noble. 2000a. *A Manual for Interpreting Community Heritage for Tourism.* Training and Technology Transfer Program, Canadian Universities Consortium Urban Environmental Management Project at the Asian Institute of Technology.

Jamieson, W. and A. Noble. 2000b. *A Manual for Sustainable Tourism Destination Management.* Training and Technology Transfer Program, Canadian Universities Consortium Urban Environmental Management Project at the Asian Institute of Technology.

Chapter 13

Computer Visualization and DTM: Historic Resource Management and Design

Richard M. Levy

INTRODUCTION

Computer visualization technology can play an important role in the tourism industry, both in site design and management. Seeing a computer model of a project before it is built can strengthen efforts to preserve important historic sites and create new destination locations (e.g., museums, parks, and interpretive centers) (Liggett and Jepson, 1993; Boland and Johnson, 1996). Once a model exists, relevant information can be incorporated into a comprehensive database that provides tourists, operators, and planners with valuable online decision support (Brenner, 1998; Hamit, 1998; Benckendorff and Black, 2000; see also http://www.bahamas.com). In addition, this technology can clarify complex design issues and thereby provide a medium for public education, avoiding unnecessary opposition and delays caused by unclear or poorly executed ideas.

For communities with an established tourism industry, a virtual model of a town, city, or region can act as a management framework that helps operators and governments better use scarce resources such as public transportation, utilities, and communication products. As an additional benefit, simulations in virtual space may also enhance communication among all parties interested in tourism destination management. Computer visualization technology offers significant

Community Destination Management in Developing Economies
© 2006 by The Haworth Press, Inc. All rights reserved.
doi:10.1300/5140_14

tools for the design and management of towns, cities, and sites dependent on tourism. In this chapter, two case studies will highlight how computer visualization technology can be used in historic resource management and urban design.

THE TOOLS

For more than 15 years, computer technology has reshaped the process of design. Many of the activities of engineers, architects, industrial designers, and creators of graphic content are now inseparable from a host of computer applications. CAD (computer aided design), GIS (geographic information systems), and VR (virtual reality) are now being used to assist urban and architectural design, interactive museum displays, and archaeological investigations (Davis, 1997; Novitski, 1998; Bocchi, 1999; see also http://www.virtualmuseum.ca). These technologies are now filtering down to local government officials, city planners, hotel operators, and tourism destination managers. However, the application of these technologies is sporadic in many areas of planning, due in part to a lack of expertise and resources needed for implementation. To master many of these computer applications still requires many years of dedication, and a split still exists between those who manage a project and those who regularly access the data on which policy is built (Sullivan, 1997). This split between the technician and the manager has tended to discourage the creative use of these digital tools for communicating ideas and exploring alternative design scenarios. Instead, computer visualization technology often is seen merely as a graphic tool, needed only for securing permits or promoting a project after a design has been approved. Until technology and decision processes can evolve in tandem, computer visualization will remain relegated to the realm of the technician's desktop.

THE PROMISE OF TECHNOLOGY

For local communities, nongovernmental organizations, and government agencies, an accurate model of a proposed development can focus energy on areas of common concern and create a level playing field. Though no guarantee exists that computer visualization will reduce the time of community consultation, this process can lead to greater clarity of ideas, which will reduce the potential for the misunderstandings that traditionally delay projects. In addition, agreement concerning the proper course of action for designing the physical environment may be difficult to obtain (Nassar, 1997). Agreement as to what is aesthetically pleasing is normative, culturally bounded, and subject to change with time. How locations look does matter and, in some cases, appearance can be the deciding factor for the acceptance of a proposed project. However, if new technology is to become an integral part of the planning process it must go beyond the visual and offer a window into other factors, such as databases that address demography, economic factors, transportation, and a range of municipal services from utilities to emergency medical services and health.

Locations with a sense of place and historic character will attract more tourists than everyday places created to serve perfunctory needs. City centers designed with greater sensitivity to the visual experience and to ease of navigation are more likely to hold a tourist's interest. In an attempt to capitalize on growing interest in recreational shopping, some communities have gone to the extreme of downtown and mall themes to attract visitors—but architectural guidelines laid down to create uniformity can result in a manufactured look.

Communities who are fortunate to have a historic downtown should maintain and preserve their unique cultural heritage rather than embark on the promotion and development of an overused advertising cliché. By establishing an Internet presence, archaeological and historic locations can be presented as interactive sites, hosting a variety of media. Streaming audio, video, quick-timeVR (QTVR), and interactive three-dimensional worlds on a Web site can all be used to educate the public on the importance of archaeological sites as cultural resources (Boland and Johnson, 1996; Hower and Parmley, 1996; Purcell, 1996; Benckendorff and Black, 2000; see also http://www.virtualmuseum.ca). A competitive advantage can be gained by using computer visualization technology to advertise, effectively building a community's visitation. In addition, a virtual world can be explored, providing would-be tourists with a powerful trip-planning tool. Museums, restaurants, and hotels can all be investigated prior to leaving home, providing reassurance that faraway destinations will be worth visiting. In a marketplace competing for tourists, improvements in communication can add an important competitive advantage.

THE FUTURE: A QUESTION
OF IMPLEMENTATION

A growing number of cities are using computer visualization technology to plan their downtowns. New York, Los Angeles, Philadelphia, and Berlin have all built computer models of their business cores that can be experienced in virtual space (Liggett and Jepson, 1993; Mahoney, 1997; Brenner, 1998; Hamit, 1998). Cities with rich histories, such as Bologna, Italy, have used this technology to present their city on a historical continuum, demonstrating how virtual worlds can preserve and chronicle a vast record of development over time (Bocchi, 1999).

If computer visualization technology is to contribute to the decision-making process, applications must be readily accessible on the computer desktops, laptops, and personal digital assistants (PDAs) along with other personal productivity software. With universal access from a Web browser, a communication style that supports the use of virtual three-dimensional technology may finally be possible. These technological advancements allow the development of a planning approach that includes all key stakeholders as a normal part of decision making (Levy, 1998).

One issue that must be considered in the implementation of new technology is how to use visualization to support good planning practices. Property ownership and historical and legal precedent can place complex constraints on the planning process. When they are detrimental to a community's general plan, the demands of individual projects must give way to common concerns. Sharing knowledge over the Internet about potential projects and plans may help build consensus toward a common vision.

PHIMAI: BUILDING INTEREST
IN HISTORIC SITES

Historic Background

A computer reconstruction of the temple site in Phimai, Thailand, is one case study that highlights the potential uses of computer visualization technology as a tool in heritage resource management (see Figure 13.1). A United Nations World Heritage Site, this walled

FIGURE 13.1. Computer model of the temple site at Phimai.

complex of reconstructed temples, libraries, and ancillary structures is considered the most important Khmer monument in Thailand. Located 60 kilometers south of the modern capital of Nakhon Ratchasima (Korat), Phimai was a center of royal patronage for Suryavarman II (AD 1113-1150) and Jayavaryman VII (AD 1181-1219). The site was first inventoried by Etienne Aymonier in 1901. Reconstruction, begun in 1964 by the Thailand Fine Arts Department under the auspices of Prince Yachai Chitrabongse, was completed in 1969 (Siribhadra and Moore, 1992).

Computer Modeling of Historic Sites

I built the model of the temple site to include an educational video and Web site in order to promote Phimai for tourism. In 1999, an initial temple site visit was made to collect data and discuss the scope of the modeling effort with the museum staff at Phimai and with Dr. Walter Jamieson, who at that time was the director of the urban management program at the Asian Institute of Technology. The computer model of the temple site began as a demonstration project to illustrate the value of new media in the promotion of a historic site. During the course of constructing the computer model, it became apparent that the model could also be used as a vehicle for communicating ideas about the temple site's reconstruction.

In the restoration of any tourist site, models offer archaeologists and museum curators a noninvasive environment for testing various reconstruction scenarios. Phimai's galleries and naves because of centuries of neglect are currently in a state of partial ruin. By extrapolating from knowledge of the vault architecture of other temple complexes in Thailand and Cambodia it was possible to show how the site may have looked in the twelfth century. This model, whose development is an ongoing process, could aid archaeologists and art historians in the consideration of other possible architectural interpretations in preparation for future reconstruction efforts. Future research aims to use computer modeling to analyze the construction technology of the temple complex at Phimai. Virtual testing of sections of the galleries and temples may reveal the distribution of forces in these stone structures. In addition, by showing how early builders constructed this complex, this structural analysis in virtual space will provide museum curators and archaeologists with an understanding of how to reconstruct areas of the temple complex that are in disrepair or have the potential to collapse.

For this historic site, images and animations based on the model of the temple site will be used as part of the museum's education program. In addition, images and QTVR movies will be placed on a national Web site sponsored by the Thailand Fine Arts Department. The Web site will provide a virtual tour of all of the major temple sites in Thailand. The model could also be used to create a VR environment of the temple grounds. A virtual environment would give students and members of the public the opportunity to explore the temple grounds from any Internet access point in the world. As an educational armature, this computer model could be used to host a wide variety of information about culture, dance, music, and religious practices.

Virtual Worlds: A Tool in the Preservation Strategy

Virtual space can show ruined sites as complete architectural forms without endangering archeological data from these sensitive sites (Forte and Siliotti, 1997). Communities have a tendency to reconstruct ruins in order to make them safer and more attractive to tourists. In the process of rebuilding sites, existing remains may be destroyed. A virtual representation, on the other hand, leaves the site intact, and even offers the potential for alternative interpretations to be viewed. Virtual sites can also protect historically important archaeological remains from destruction caused by excessive visitation (Koprowski, 1997). In the future, virtual models may be the only means by which the public can experience certain historical sites, particularly sites with safety risks or where human traffic poses a serious danger to the integrity of the structure.

BANGKOK NOI:
PROMOTING A COMMON VISION

As part of a United Nations Education, Scientific and Cultural Organization (UNESCO)-supported program to promote regional development initiatives in urban planning, a workshop was held in April 1999 concerning the future of Bangkok's historic canals. The Khlong Bangkok Noi and Khlong Om Canals, located a few kilometers north of the city, preserve many of the special qualities associated with Bangkok when it was known as the "Venice of the East" (Wiessner and Levy, 2000).

The unplanned nature of Bangkok's urban development has resulted in an almost complete and irretrievable loss of open spaces. Consequently, Bangkok's residents today are faced with few parks in the more urbanized area, with only two major parks in the central city. Unregulated urban sprawl within a radius of approximately 100 kilometers from Bangkok's city center makes it extremely time-consuming to escape the hustle and bustle of downtown. The middle class is expanding, and demand for recreational space is expected to increase along with residents' greater disposable income and leisure time. One consequence is the substantial residential growth that has been occurring in Nonthaburi as more and more of the middle class buy homes along the canal.

Because scenic qualities are at risk of degradation, discussion focuses on how to preserve the region as a tourist and recreational area. Unregulated development in recent decades has resulted in a number of new buildings being added to the scenic canalscapes. Industrial and apartment buildings, electric utilities, and highway bridges now can be seen alongside traditional wood stilt homes and wooden piers. Without future regulation, the present rate of new development will seriously mar these areas for tourists, as is already the case in some of the more established urbanized areas of Bangkok (Wiessner and Levy, 2000).

Building Consensus: A Role for Computer Modeling

The development of proper coordination among the various governmental agencies and other agencies of concern proved to be a major challenge in the initial stages of this project. The provincial government, several independent municipal governments, and a number of smaller, rural administrative subdistricts (tambon) have a role in the area. Each of these jurisdictions is presided over by an independently elected official. A successful planning initiative would require close cooperation between all levels of government. During early meetings with government representatives, lack of coordination and little common vision had resulted in vaguely defined and often contradictory objectives.

To reach a common understanding of the planning project, a three-dimensional computer model was created to improve communication among agencies by illustrating the potential recreational and tourism value of the area. The modeling process began with the compilation of a list of the concerns regarding canal restoration from government officials and experts who attended workshops and meetings on the future of this area. The list of visual elements of key concern formed the basis of two possible scenarios. The first scenario (left figure) showed a portion of the canal as it might look in the future if no regulatory guidance were in place (Figure 13.2). This first alternative would offer decision makers a view of an unregulated future to contemplate. The alternative scenario (right figure) would consider how the same section of the canal might look if specific development controls were in place (Table 13.1). These controls would limit use, building form, and canal treatments along the water's edge (see Figure 13.2). The goal of any proposed bylaws or architectural guidelines would be to encourage the preservation of the canal's visual character. Limiting the massing of buildings to two-story residential structures would maintain canal views of the trees and foliage immediately behind and adjacent to existing development. In addition, using local materials as well as architecture that relies on traditional building would result in

FIGURE 13.2. View of development along the canal.

TABLE 13.1. Proposed design guidelines used in constructing the two scenarios.

Without Regulatory Guidance	With Regulatory Guidance
Permitted structures:	*Permitted structures:*
1. Apartments 2. Industrial buildings 3. Residential homes 4. Highway bridges	1. No apartment structures would be permitted. 2. Industrial and temporary buildings would not be a permitted use. 3. Residential buildings permitted: architectural guidelines would encourage use of traditional materials and building forms. 4. Construction of highway bridges would not be permitted along scenic portions of the canal.
Landscaping:	
1. Concrete retaining walls	1. Encouragement of the use of more compatible forms such as earth berms 2. Use of overflow areas in case of high canal levels

new development sympathetic to the existing traditional architecture. Finally, barring construction of highway bridges over the canal would help preserve vistas and eliminate a major source of sound pollution in the immediate area. Adopting these measures would help protect the area as a significant tourism attraction.

A Strategy for Model Building

Rather than modeling a specific portion of the canal, prototypical buildings and landscape features were assembled along a virtual model of a one-mile portion of the canal (illustrated in Figure 13.2). This approach guarantees that while watching a 20-second animation created from the model the viewer experiences all of the key elements in each of the two scenarios. The specific sources of features in the model were photos and videos taken early in 1999 from a water taxi on the canal. The model was built and rendered with computer applications used in the production of computer-generated animation and special effects in film and video. The strategy for constructing the model was to utilize simple geometric primitives with applied image maps. Since not all stakeholders were able to visit the site, the use of virtual reality made it possible to generate photorealistic views along the canal that everyone could access. This helped avoid possible misinterpretation of the landscape and architectural features of the canal based on lack of information. It also served to refresh the memories of those who had seen the site. In addition, this model can easily serve as a test bed for viewing future proposals, through the simple addition or deletion of elements. Output from the first test model was reviewed using a Web site established for the project. Both images and interactive panoramas of possible future canalscapes were placed on this Web site (Levy, 2000). Changes could then be made and the Web site updated as new images were produced. For the final review, a PowerPoint presentation with embedded animations was also created, along with a supporting video and Web site. The two views generated from the computer model (Figure 13.2) show the canal without regulatory guidance (left) with the proposed design guidelines in place (right).

The model was presented to government officials in a Steering Committee session on March 21, 2000. Having a visual representation of the development scenarios made it easier for officials to discuss the future of the area during the weeks that followed. In general, having seen the model, the concerned agencies felt easier in advocating ideas. The use of computer visualization technology not only promoted new ways of thinking about the areas but also broadened the political scope and acceptance of alternative approaches. Following the presentation, all 16 local governments of the canal landscape and the provincial government of Nonthaburi decided to establish cooperative mechanisms among themselves to jointly identify a sustainable development approach for Thailand's last urban canal landscape. In an official ceremony on April 27, 2000, the UN-HABITAT Urban Management Programme encouraged the governments to support their initiative with financial funding, and a Memorandum of Understanding was signed (Wiessner and Levy, 2000).

CONCLUSION

Computer visualization technology can play an important role in protecting areas important to tourism. It can demonstrate vividly the potential damage that can occur if cooperative action is not taken. In the example of the preservation efforts for Khlong canals, visual representation made it easier to arrive at a positive common agreement to deal with this threatened aesthetic and historical resource.

For historic sites of great cultural significance, computer visualization technology can be enlisted to help protect and promote irreplaceable cultural assets. Virtual models can be used to plan conservation efforts. Just as important, virtual models can be used to enhance the visitor's experience by providing animations and VR environments that provide the cultural context and background of an historic site. Because much of this content can be viewed over the Internet, real potential exists for creating virtual tours complete with guides. Providing tourists with the ability to preview and plan a cultural tour can only help local communities stay competitive in this very aggressive industry.

REFERENCES

Benckendorff, P.J. and M.L. Black. 2000. Destination marketing on the Internet: A case study of Australian Regional Tourism Authorities. *The Journal of Tourism Studies* 11(1): 11-21.

Bocchi, F. 1999. "The 4D virtual museum of the city of Bologna, Italy." Paper presented at SIGGRAPH International Conference on Computer Graphics and Interactive Techniques, August 8-13, Los Angeles, California.

Boland, P. and C. Johnson. 1996. Archaeology as computer visualization: 'Virtual tours' of Dudley Castle c. 1550. In *British Museum Occasional Papers*, vol. 114 (pp. 227-233). London: The British Museum.

Brenner, T. 1998. *Echtzeit: Integrative Kommunikation.* Available online at: <http://www.echtzeit.de>.

Davis, B. 1997. The future of the past. *Scientific American,* August: 89-90.

Forte, M. and A. Siliotti. 1997. *Virtual Archaeology.* New York: Harry N. Abrams Inc.

Hamit F. 1998. The urban simulation lab's image-based model of the future of Los Angeles. *Advanced Imaging* 13(7): 32-36.

Hower, R. and J. Parmley. 1996. The interactive studio: Collaborative multimedia projects that have revealed the Mesa Verde National Park, the Anasazi culture and cliff dwellings, and are currently illuminating the fossil life of the United States National Parks. In *British Museum Occasional Papers*, vol. 114 (pp. 141-147). London: The British Museum.

Koprowski, G. 1997. VR artist re-creates Paleolithic times. *Wired,* February. Available online at: <http://www.wired.com/news/culture/0,1284,2199,00.html>.

Levy, R. 1998. Information technology and the planning profession: Where is it taking us? *Plan Canada* 38(5): 24-29.

Levy, R. 2000. Towards a sustainable preservation strategy for the Khlong Bangkok Noi/Khlong Om Canal area, Nonthaburi, Thailand. Available online at: <http://www.acs.ucalgary.ca/~rmlevy/Noi/index.html>.

Liggett, R. and W.H. Jepson. 1993. An integrated environment for urban simulation. In R.E. Klosterman and S.P. French (Eds.), *Proceedings of the Third International Conference on Computers in Urban Planning and Urban Management* (pp. 565-583). Atlanta, GA: Georgia Institute of Technology.

Mahoney, D.P. 1997. Philadelphia 2000. *Computer Graphics World* 20(6): 30-33.

Nassar, J. 1997. *The Evaluative Image of the City.* Thousand Oaks, CA: Sage.

Novitski, B.J. 1998. Reconstructing lost architecture. *Computer Graphics World* 21(12): 24.

Purcell, P. 1996. Museum 2000: A multimedia prospect. In *British Museum Occasional Papers,* vol. 114 (pp. 119-125). London: The British Museum.

Siribhadra, S. and E. Moore. 1992. *Places of the Gods, Khmer Art and Architecture of Thailand.* Bangkok: River Books.

Sullivan, A.C. 1997. Holdouts to converts. *Architecture* 2(86): 126-128.

Wiessner, G. and R. Levy. 2000. "Application of Computer Visualization Techniques in Project Negotiation: The Nonthaburi Canal Development Project in Thailand." Paper presented at the Seventeenth EAROPH Congress, October 11-13, Onyang, Korea.

Chapter 14

The Role of Festivals and Events in Community Tourism Destination Management

Jerome Agrusa

INTRODUCTION

One of the fastest-growing areas of the burgeoning tourism industry is festivals and events tourism, which has become a very important part of community destination management (Neirotti, 2003). Large-scale events designed to attract large numbers of spectators can funnel thousands or even millions of dollars into a local economy (Mules and Faulkner, 1996). However, smaller, participatory events, such as festivals, can also be advantageous, particularly for smaller cities or less populated regions. Since participatory events often make use of existing infrastructure and volunteer labor, they can be relatively inexpensive to host, and can yield high benefit-to-cost ratios (Allenby, 2000). Furthermore, participatory festivals and events have been shown to be an effective way to attract new visitors to an area and to generate return visits. Such events target consumers who seek opportunities to share their holidays with others who are also interested in the festival or event (Green and Chalip, 1998).

Small communities around the world are developing new festivals and events to enhance community development and economic prosperity. On the other hand, some festivals and events have a long tradition of community involvement and played an important role in the local culture and social framework prior to any recognition of the

Community Destination Management in Developing Economies
© 2006 by The Haworth Press, Inc. All rights reserved.
doi:10.1300/5140_15

potential economic impacts of visitor expenditure on the community (McDonnell, et al., 1999).

Because festivals and events rely on enthusiastic participation, event planning does not work best with a "top down" management approach that tries to impose practices on to a community, region, or institution. The planning for these events works best from a bottom-up management approach that considers individual and community needs first. Placing the needs of the host population first when marketing a festival or event in a destination is an example of responsible tourism (Seaton and Bennett, 1996).

Putting the community in control of event development means that local people have a say in how they are represented to others. Such an approach to festivals or events encourages tourists to "get off the road" in order to encounter the authentic traditions of a culture. In the process, festivals and events also encourage local residents to engage with the tourists who come to participate, because they were involved in the planning and marketing from the beginning.

A well-managed festival or event has the potential to diversify a destination's economic base, and can provide incentives to preserve a destination's special character and artifacts.

CULTURAL FESTIVALS AND EVENTS

A festival may be defined as "a ritualized break from routine that defines certain values in an atmosphere of joy and fellowship" (Horne, 1989, p. 62). Potential economic benefits aside, many reasons can be given for why communities organize events. These reasons include enhancing or preserving local culture and history and providing local recreation and leisure opportunities. Festivals also offer the potential to showcase a region and to foster local organizational development, leadership, and networking, all of which are critical underpinnings of community-based tourism development. Festivals are a powerful way to share with visitors what is distinctive about communities. Getz (1997) and McDonnell et al. (1999) suggest that these events can play an important role in the development of community and regional identity as well as reflect the lifestyle choices made by residents.

When developing authentic cultural festivals and events, it is the destination's responsibility to place the aspect of the culture it is exhibiting in its historical and cultural context. This can be done in a variety of ways: charts, diagrams, commentary delivered through earphones, explanatory audiovisual programs, docents who conduct tours, booklets and catalogs, educational programs, lectures, and/or performances. The goal of all of these approaches is to engage tourists while providing them with accurate information. Obviously, determining the appropriate context can be a challenge, particularly when real, living people are included in displays.

The sustainability of the festival or event depends in large part on guarding against commercial exploitation or the enhancement of one categorical resource at the expense of others. Derrett emphasizes that festivals are at the interface of three dynamic features of regional communities: the *community,* representing the sense of place of residents; the *exchange sector* of tourism, representing the visitors; and the elements of *image and identity* that reflect the message received in the marketplace (Derrett, 2000).

Evidence suggests that as festivals and events grow and attract more tourists, commoditization takes place. "Commoditization is a strange word," writes Allenby (2000). "Frequently found in Marxist discourse, it means the process by which market capitalism changes things that were previously not regarded as economic goods into something with a price, and, concomitantly, part of the economy." Industry demographics indicate increasing activity in almost all areas of support infrastructure that serve the tourist's consumer segment. Bolton (1998) notes that commoditization is "a capitalist driven mechanism that sees an opportunity for profit in natural and cultural resources." No doubt many tourists very much want to learn about and move among the world's inventory of historic areas, sites, and related settings, festivals, and events.

CASE STUDY: MARDI GRAS

Some of the largest community festivals in the United States are held in the state of Louisiana. The largest of these is the New Orleans Mardi Gras. The second largest festival is the Mardi Gras held in Lafayette, a city with a population of only 110,257 (City-Data.com, 2000). Travel and tourism has become Louisiana's second largest industry and has helped to stabilize the local economy, which was once dominated by the petroleum industry. Over the past few years, tourism in Louisiana has increased significantly. In large measure, this is due to the increasing popularity of the large number of festivals and special events that the state holds every year (University of New Orleans, 1999). Many of these festivals, particularly Mardi Gras, revolve around the tradition and culture of the state.

This case study will explore the economic scale of the Lafayette Mardi Gras and will discuss some of the other types of economic impacts relevant to the determination of the economic significance of a festival to the local community.

The Background of the Lafayette Mardi Gras

The parish of Lafayette is the focal point of southwestern Louisiana, a region also known as Acadiana. Acadiana is particularly rich in unique local culture; it received its name when French-speaking Acadians from Nova Scotia refused to swear allegiance to the British crown in 1755 and were forced from their homeland (National Parks Service and Parks, Canada, 1992). Those who were exiled made the journey to the Louisiana territory to find new homes along the fertile bayous and prairies of South Louisiana. The culture and traditions of Lafayette remain uniquely Cajun (derived from Acadian). The city has a large number of French-speaking inhabitants and is renowned for its Cajun and Creole cuisine. The area also has numerous festivals that are unique to its Cajun, Creole, and German heritage.

In the early 1800s, the custom of Courir du Mardi Gras (Running of Fat Tuesday) developed in the rural towns of Acadiana: Mamou, Iota, Eunice, and Church Point (Hardy, 1998; Greater New Orleans Tourist and Convention Commission, 1966). Each year, masked riders on horseback rode a specified route, led by a captain carrying a white flag. The captain would ride up to a farmhouse along the route to ask permission for the Mardi Gras to come up to the house. The captain would then lower the flag once permission was granted. "This signaled the costumed riders to fire up at top speed, dismount to dance, cavort and sing a 'beggin' song' for ingredients for the gumbo to be enjoyed that night at the fais-do-do" (Mamalakis, 1992, p. B2). When the farmer indicated the chicken or guinea pig to be given to the gumbo, a mad scramble ensued. Once the fowl was caught, the maskers danced and sang, and then left to repeat their performance at the next farmer's house. The run was complete once the riders returned back to town, where a large gumbo was cooked with the food they had picked up along the way. This custom of running is still observed in some small towns around Lafayette, and keeps the Cajun folk culture alive (Mamalakis, 1992).

The first written record of a formal Mardi Gras celebration, complete with a ball and a parade, occurs in 1869. This year is well known for its colorful and dramatic Mardi Gras King, Judge George Armand Martin, a physician, planter, judge, gentleman, and scholar (Mamalakis, 1992, p. B2). His reign as King Attakapas is one that is remembered to this day.

That year, the city of Lafayette held a memorable parade, complete with floats and revelers from all the neighboring towns (Mamalakis, 1992). But for some time afterward, no public observance of Mardi Gras was held in Lafayette until a local teacher sparked a revival of Mardi Gras observance in 1927. A highschool carnival ball was planned along with a citywide carnival celebration that restored the observance of Mardi Gras throughout the city. In 1934, The Southwest Louisiana Mardi Gras Association was formed to assist in the citywide observance of Mardi Gras by establishing Mardi Gras krewes, balls, and pageant celebrations (Mamalakis, 1992).

The celebration of Mardi Gras is rich in the customs, traditions, legend, and folklore of the area. The people who were born in the area as well as those who have moved there and call it home have adopted the spirit of Mardi Gras and enthusiastically continue the popular Mardi Gras tradition.

Community Value of Mardi Gras

Some researchers speak of community attachment to an event (Fredline and Faulkner, 2000a). Celebrations have been likened to "glue" that can bind a community together, an "elixir" that can invigorate community spirit, and a "renewing experience" that keeps the community relevant and responsive to social needs (Derrett, 2000). These metaphors appear to be particularly apt for the Lafayette Mardi Gras, which provides an opportunity for residents and visitors to participate, for a brief time, in a themed celebration of the community's historic and present identity.

Community attitudes appear to be positive toward the Mardi Gras festivities. One must of course be mindful that different members of the community have different value systems that influence their ways of perceiving reality (Fredline and Faulkner, 2000b), and that this complicates any claim that an event "represents" the cultural milieu and values of a host community (Williams et al., 1995). For the majority of Lafayette residents, however, Mardi Gras seems to be an opportunity to enjoy the mild weather of early spring (pleasantly cool for those who live in the hot, southern United States, and a warm respite for those who live in the north, where winter can last until May) with friends and family.

Some people choose to participate in the organizations called *krewes*. The krewes are secret societies, originally composed of the upper classes of society, who organize debutante balls and support many charities anonymously. During the event, the members and guests are entertained with theatrical plays that introduce elaborately dressed debutantes, and the live music and dancing last until dawn. Krewe members also organize and participate as costumed paraders in the annual carnival. The theatrical plays showcase the history of Mardi Gras and the founding fathers of that particular krewe. The highlight of the ball is the announcing of the Queen, who will reign throughout the Mardi Gras season.

The Lafayette area currently has about 25 nonparading krewes and 16 parading krewes, with an average membership of 125. When interviewed, many krewe members say they get together to put on the parade to remember the tradition, culture, and fun of Mardi Gras—the cultural event of the Acadian year. Others enjoy the Mardi Gras weekend for its abundance of good food, drinks, live entertainment, and Mardi Gras parades.

Throughout the four days of the festival, thousands of people experience the century-old tradition that has evolved into modern-day Mardi Gras. When krewe members were asked how many balls they had attended during the year 2000 Mardi Gras season, the response was an average of 2.4 balls, with 17.0 percent of the respondents stating that they had attended four or more balls. This indicates a large degree of community involvement in the Mardi Gras. Virtually every local business that deals directly with the public incorporates Mardi Gras into their advertising.

Locals support their community by offering services not regularly offered at other times of the year. Vendors set up booths along parade routes to accommodate the thousands of Mardi Gras goers. These vendors offer beverages and food items not normally included on their menu. This allows the public to enjoy their Mardi Gras experience and the vendors to earn some extra revenue. Such activities help to increase the economic scale of the festival.

The attitude of the public is upbeat and positive. Residents enjoy meeting new people and creating a friendly atmosphere for visitors. The Mardi Gras festival creates a temporary community in which new values and art can be explored as joyful community practice. It is a statewide holiday, and schools and businesses take vacation time so that everyone can enjoy the festivities. It has been written that festivals provide a mechanism to bring diverse factions of the community into a shared experience (Craik, 1997, p. 135). This certainly appears to be the case for the Lafayette Mardi Gras.

Economic Impacts of Mardi Gras

As defined by Getz, the economic scale of an event is measured by the total size of the expenditures associated with the event. One way to express this is to estimate total event attendance and total expenditure by event consumers and organizers (Getz, 1987). The economic scale of Mardi Gras can be determined by adding the amount of money spent by krewe members and guests for the balls and parades to the amount of money spent by tourists who visit and participate in the Lafayette Mardi Gras.

In the year 2000, more than a million people (1,039,000) viewed the four days of parades in Lafayette (Dwyer, Agrusa, and Coats, 2001). This was an increase of 8 percent more than the 1999 Mardi Gras parade attendance. These aggregate figures include those persons who attend more than one parade, and include locals as well as visitors. The city of Lafayette police department estimated that local attendance over the four days of the parades in 2000 was 281,250, including multiple parade attendance. Given Lafayette's population of 110,257, each local resident spent 2.5 days attending parades. This figure seems to be reasonable in view of community involvement in the Mardi Gras. Once local attendance is accounted for, the total "tourist" days associated with the Mardi Gras are 758,300 (Dwyer, Agrusa, and Coats, 2001).

Several categories of spending are associated with the Lafayette Mardi Gras. Each will be considered in turn. A sales tax of 2.0 percent is assessed on all spending on goods and services, which contributes to the tax revenue (collected by the Lafayette Parish School Board Sales Tax Division) to the City of Lafayette. Hotel revenue is subject to a 10.5 percent tax, a figure that includes the 2.0 percent sales tax that goes to the city and a 3.0 percent Bed Tax that goes to the Lafayette Convention and Visitors Commission (LCVC) and is allocated for the promotion of tourism in the area.

The total spending associated with the Lafayette carnival parades in 2000 was $55,892,400. This estimate should be regarded as a maximum amount since not all Mardi Gras related purchases of goods and services will be transacted locally or will contribute to the city's taxation revenue. The estimated percentage of items purchased locally is based on a survey of local businesses. Estimation of the "leakages" from visitor expenditure is very difficult to measure accurately.

After adjusting for expenditures made outside of the local area, the net local expenditure in 2000 was estimated to be $44,388,000. This generated about $888,000 in direct taxes for the city of Lafayette, including $31,000 to the LCVC. Since the expenditure associated with Mardi Gras affects business activity in the region, this estimate of economic scale provides an upper limit to the economic significance of the festival for Lafayette Parish.

It is not just visitor expenditure that is relevant to the in-scope expenditure estimation. If an event causes residents to spend from their savings, this additional expenditure counts toward in-scope expenditure as long as the expenditure would otherwise have been saved or spent outside of the area—and is therefore additional to what residents would have spent in the course of ordinary life. Thus, the Mardi Gras festival can retain money locally that would otherwise be spent elsewhere and can generate resident spending over and above normal levels. Furthermore, if residents "holiday at home" during the festival rather than leave the area, then a proportion of their normal expenditure can also be regarded as in scope.

Several other types of economic impacts are not taken into account in traditional economic impact assessment. These impacts result from expenditure injections associated with events but are not directly related to the in-scope expenditures of visitors, organizers, and sponsors. These "other" economic impacts of Mardi Gras can include new business development, investment induced into the local area, net benefits and costs to local communities, and the long-term benefits to tourism promotion of the destination (Dwyer et al., 2000).

In addition to these other types of economic impacts, many more benefits and costs associated with a festival exist that are not objectively quantifiable. Questions about the costs and benefits of the Lafayette Mardi Gras from environmental, social, and cultural perspectives are certainly relevant (Burns et al., 1986; Burgan and Mules, 2000). These costs might include grants from within the parish that could have been used for other purposes; construction and demolition expenditure; planning, marketing, and operating costs; externalities such as loss of amenity, costs to government agencies (police, fire, health, waste disposal, etc.) that can be attributed to the festival; costs of damage to private property caused by the event; costs of crime associated with the festival; and traffic congestion, noise disturbance, etc. Benefits might include grants received from outside the area; an enhanced sense of community well-being and community pride; validation of community groups, expansion of cultural perspectives, and enhancement of cultural traditions; and enhancement of social cohesion (McDonnell et al., 1999).

While some researchers have attempted to determine the social worth of an event by assigning monetary values to all costs (economic, social, environmental, etc.) that residents are willing to bear to host the event (e.g., Burns et al., 1986), Getz (2000) poses the important question: What is lost if an event disappears? In the present context, the loss of the Lafayette Mardi Gras would deny residents a large element of their sense of place.

With visitors urged to "do as the locals do," the Lafayette Mardi Gras provides an opportunity to explore the values, interests, and aspirations of visitors. It can also help to answer the following questions: What formal and informal cultural experiences are shared by hosts and guests (Tiyce and Dimmock, 2000)? Is the Lafayette Mardi Gras molding culture for tourism and tourists or molding tourism and tourists for culture—or both (Craik, 1997, p. 122)? An annual festival such as the Lafayette Mardi Gras can serve as an ongoing case study of host and guest values and sources of change.

CONCLUDING OBSERVATIONS

Experts tell us that festivals and events can, if properly developed, offer a life-changing experience for tourists, introducing them to new cultures that provide enriched visions of the world. Festivals and events are now seen as an essential aspect of tourism destination management. These events, if developed without regard to sustainability, can reduce a local culture to a set of crass stereotypes and two-dimensional cutouts poorly understood by visitors. In other words, unbridled or poorly managed development of festivals and events might turn something unique and life-changing into something trivial. However, if nurtured properly for sustainability and enthusiastic community involvement, festivals and events can allow tourists to leave a destination with wonderful memories and a deeper appreciation of the community that has hosted them.

The theme that runs through this chapter is the interrelationship between the economic and various other impacts (social, cultural, and environmental) that any festival or major community event will have on a host community. That is to say, the economic scale of an event or festival, and its overall contribution to a community, cannot be assessed in isolation from the social and cultural context in which the festival is held. After all, it is community attachment to a festival that gives rise to and sustains the economic effects in the first place.

REFERENCES

Allenby, B. (2000). The commoditization of nature. Available online at: <http://www.att.com/ehs/ind_ecology/articles/commoditization.html>.

Bolton, R. (1998). The appropriation and commoditization of Niagara Falls as reflected in environmental legislation and the tourist industry. Available online at: <http://www.courses.rochester.edu/foster/ANT226/Archive/Fall98/16.html>.

Burgan, B. and T. Mules (2000). Estimating the impact of events—Sampling frame issues in identifying event related expenditure. In J. Allen, R. Harris, L. Jago, and J. Veal (Eds.), *Events Beyond 2000: Setting the Agenda.* Proceedings of Conference on Event Evaluation, Research and Education, Sydney, Australia: July.

Burns, J.P.A, J. Hatch, and T. Mules (Eds.) (1986). *The Adelaide Grand Prix: The Impact of a Special Event.* Adelaide, Australia: University of Adelaide.

City-Data.com (2000). Lafayette, Louisiana. Available online at: http://www.city-data.com/city/Lafayette-Louisiana.html.

Craik, J. (1997). Touring cultures—Transformation of travel and theory. In C. Rojek and J. Urry (Eds.), *The Culture of Tourism* (p. 1-135). London: Routledge.

Derrett, R. (2000). Can festivals brand community cultural development and cultural tourism simultaneously? In J. Allen, R. Harris, L. Jago, and J. Veal (Eds.), *Events Beyond 2000: Setting the Agenda.* Proceedings of Conference on Event Evaluation, Research and Education, Sydney, Australia: July.

Dwyer, L., J. Agrusa, and W. Coats (2001). Economic scale of a community event: The Lafayette Mardi Gras. *Pacific Tourism Review* 5(3): 167-179.

Dwyer, L., R. Mellor, N. Mistilis, and T. Mules (2000). A framework for assessing "tangible" and "intangible" impacts of events and conventions. *Event Management* 6: 175-189.

Fredline, E. and B. Faulkner (2000a). Community perceptions of the impacts of events. In J. Allen, R. Harris, L. Jago and J. Veal (Eds.), *Events Beyond 2000: Setting the Agenda.* Proceedings of Conference on Event Evaluation, Research and Education, Sydney, Australia: July.

Fredline, E. and B. Faulkner (2000b). Host community reactions: A cluster analysis. *Annals of Tourism Research* 27: 764-785.

Getz, D. (1987). Event tourism: Evaluating the impacts. In B. Ritchie and C. Goeldner (Eds.), *Travel, Tourism and Hospitality Research: A Handbook for Managers and Researchers,* Second edition (pp. 437-450). New York: John Wiley and Sons.

Getz, D. (1997). *Event Management and Event Tourism.* New York: Cognizant Communication Corporation.

Getz, D. (2000). Developing a research agenda for the event management field. In J. Allen, R. Harris, L. Jago and J. Veal (Eds.), *Events Beyond 2000: Setting the Agenda.* Proceedings of Conference on Event Evaluation, Research and Education, Sydney, Australia: July.

Greater New Orleans Tourist and Convention Commission (1966). *The Story of the New Orleans Mardi Gras* (pp. 1-2). New Orleans, LA: Author.

Green, B.C. and L. Chalip (1998). Sport tourism as the celebration of subculture. *Annals of Tourism Research* 25: 275-291.

Hardy, A. (1998). The history of Mardi Gras. *Arthur Hardy's Mardi Gras Guide* 22: 14-18.

Horne, D. (1989). *Ideas for a Nation.* Sydney: John Wiley and Sons.

Mamalakis, M. (1992). "Mardi Gras has a strong history in Lafayette." *The Daily Advertiser,* February 11, p. B2.

McDonnell I., J. Allen, and W. O'Toole. (1999). *Festival and Special Event Management.* Brisbane: John Wiley and Sons.

Mules, T. and B. Faulkner (1996). An economic perspective on special events. *Tourism Economics* 2: 107-117.

National Parks Service and Parks Canada (producer). (1992). *The Cajun Way: Echoes of Acadia* [film]. Lafayette, LA: The Jeanne Lafitte Cultural Center.

Neirotti, L.D. (2003). An introduction to sport and adventure tourism. In S. Hudson (Ed.), *Sport and Adventure Tourism* (pp. 1-25). New York: The Haworth Hospitality Press.

Seaton, T. and M. Bennett (1996). *The Marketing of Tourism Products: Concepts, Issues and Cases.* Boston: International Thompson Business Press.

Tiyce, M., and K. Dimmock. (2000). Nimbin Mardi Gras Festival: The impacts. In J. Allen, R. Harris, L. Jago and J. Veal (Eds.), *Events Beyond 2000: Setting the*

Agenda. Proceedings of Conference on Event Evaluation, Research and Education, Sydney, Australia: July.

University of New Orleans for the Louisiana Office of Tourism. (1999). *Louisiana Welcome Center visitor survey: Final report.* January. New Orleans, LA: Louisiana Office of Tourism.

Williams P., D. Hainsworth, and K. Dossa (1995). Community development and special event tourism: The Men's World Cup of Skiing at Whistler, British Columbia. *The Journal of Tourism Studies* 6: 11-20.

Index

Community Destination Management in Developing Economies
© 2006 by The Haworth Press, Inc. All rights reserved.
doi:10.1300/5140_16

THE HAWORTH HOSPITALITY PRESS®
Hospitality, Travel, and Tourism
K. S. Chon, PhD, Editor in Chief

CULTURAL TOURISM: GLOBAL AND LOCAL PERSPECTIVES edited by Greg Richards. (2007).

GAY TOURISM: CULTURE AND CONTEXT by Gordon Waitt and Kevin Markwell. (2006).

CASES IN SUSTAINABLE TOURISM: AN EXPERIENTIAL APPROACH TO MAKING DECISIONS edited by Irene M. Herremans. (2006). "As a tourism instructor and researcher, I recommend this textbook for both undergraduate and graduate students who wish to pursue their careers in parks, recreation, or tourism. The text is appropriate both for junior and senior tourism management classes and graduate classes. It is an excellent primer for understanding the fundamental concepts, issues, and real-world examples of sustainable tourism." *HwanSuk Chrus Choi, PhD, Assistant Professor, School of Hospitality and Tourism Management, University of Gueph*

COMMUNITY DESTINATION MANAGEMENT IN DEVELOPING ECONOMIES edited by Walter Jamieson. (2006). "This book is a welcome and valuable addition to the destination management literature, focusing as it does on developing economies in the Asian context. It provides an unusually comprehensive and informative overview of critical issues in the field, effectively combining well-crafted discussions of key conceptual and methodological issues with carefully selected and well-presented case studies drawn from a number of contrasting Asian destinations." *Peter Hills, PhD, Professor and Director, The Centre of Urban Planning and Environmental Management, The University of Hong Kong*

MANAGING SUSTAINABLE TOURISM: A LEGACY FOR THE FUTURE by David L. Edgell Sr. (2006). "This comprehensive book on sustainable tourism should be required reading for everyone interested in tourism. The author is masterful in defining strategies and using case studies to explain best practices in generating long-term economic return on your tourism investment." *Kurtis M. Ruf, Partner, Ruf Strategic Solutions; Author, Contemporary Database Marketing*

CASINO INDUSTRY IN ASIA PACIFIC: DEVELOPMENT, OPERATION, AND IMPACT edited by Cathy H.C. Hsu. (2006). "This book is a must-read for anyone interested in the opportunities and challenges that the proliferation of casino gaming will bring to Asia in the early twenty-first century. The economic and social consequences of casino gaming in Asia may ultimately prove to be far more significant than those encountered in the West, and this book opens the door as to what those consequences might be." *William R. Eadington, PhD, Professor of Economics and Director, Institute for the Study of Gambling and Commercial Gaming, University of Nevada, Reno*

THE GROWTH STRATEGIES OF HOTEL CHAINS: BEST BUSINESS PRACTICES BY LEADING COMPANIES by Onofre Martorell Cunill. (2006). "Informative, well-written, and up-to-date. This is one title that I shall certainly be adding to my 'must-read' list for students this year." *Tom Baum, PhD, Professor of International Tour-*

ism and Hospitality Management, The Scottish Hotel School, The University of Strathclyde, Glasgow

HANDBOOK FOR DISTANCE LEARNING IN TOURISM by Gary Williams. (2005). "This is an important book for a variety of audiences. As a resource for educational designers (and their managers) in particular, it is invaluable. The book is easy to read, and is full of practical information that can be logically applied in the design and development of flexible learning resources." *Louise Berg, MA, DipED, Lecturer in Education, Charles Sturt University, Australia*

VIETNAM TOURISM by Arthur Asa Berger. (2005). "Fresh and innovative.... Drawing upon Professor Berger's background and experience in cultural studies, this book offers an imaginative and personal portrayal of Vietnam as a tourism destination.... A very welcome addition to the field of destination studies." *Professor Brian King, PhD, Head, School of Hospitality, Tourism & Marketing, Victoria University, Australia*

TOURISM AND HOTEL DEVELOPMENT IN CHINA: FROM POLITICAL TO ECONOMIC SUCCESS by Hanqin Qiu Zhang, Ray Pine, and Terry Lam. (2005). "This is one of the most comprehensive books on China tourism and hotel development. It is one of the best textbooks for educators, students, practitioners, and investors who are interested in china tourism and hotel industry. Readers will experience vast, diversified, and past and current issues that affect every educator, student, practitioner, and investor in China tourism and hotel globally in an instant." *Hailin Qu, PhD, Full Professor and William E. Davis Distinguished Chair, School of Hotel & Restaurant Administration, Oklahoma State University*

THE TOURISM AND LEISURE INDUSTRY: SHAPING THE FUTURE edited by Klaus Weiermair and Christine Mathies. (2004). "If you need or want to know about the impact of globalization, the impact of technology, societal forces of change, the experience economy, adaptive technologies, environmental changes, or the new trend of slow tourism, you need this book. *The Tourism and Leisure Industry* contains a great mix of research and practical information." *Charles R. Goeldner, PhD, Professor Emeritus of Marketing and Tourism, Leeds School of Business, University of Colorado*

OCEAN TRAVEL AND CRUISING: A CULTURAL ANALYSIS by Arthur Asa Berger. (2004). "Dr. Berger presents an interdisciplinary discussion of the cruise industry for the thinking person. This is an enjoyable social psychology travel guide with a little business management thrown in. A great book for the curious to read a week before embarking on a first cruise or for the frequent cruiser to gain a broader insight into exactly what a cruise experience represents." *Carl Braunlich, DBA, Associate Professor, Department of Hospitality and Tourism Management, Purdue University, West Lafayette, Indiana*

STANDING THE HEAT: ENSURING CURRICULUM QUALITY IN CULINARY ARTS AND GASTRONOMY by Joseph A. Hegarty. (2003). "This text provides the genesis of a well-researched, thoughtful, rigorous, and sound theoretical framework for the enlargement and expansion of higher education programs in culinary arts and gastronomy." *John M. Antun, PhD, Founding Director, National Restaurant Institute, School of Hotel, Restaurant, and Tourism Management, University of South Carolina*

SEX AND TOURISM: JOURNEYS OF ROMANCE, LOVE, AND LUST edited by Thomas G. Bauer and Bob McKercher. (2003). "Anyone interested in or concerned about the impact of tourism on society and particularly in the developing world, should read this book. It explores a subject that has long remained ignored, almost a taboo area for many governments, institutions, and organizations. It demonstrates that the stereotyping of 'sex tourism' is too simple and travel and sex have many manifestations. The book follows its theme in an innovative and original way." *Carson L. Jenkins, PhD, Professor of International Tourism, University of Strathclyde, Glasgow, Scotland*

CONVENTION TOURISM: INTERNATIONAL RESEARCH AND INDUSTRY PERSPECTIVES edited by Karin Weber and Kye-Sung Chon. (2002). "This comprehensive book is truly global in its perspective. The text points out areas of needed research—a great starting point for graduate students, university faculty, and industry professionals alike. While the focus is mainly academic, there is a lot of meat for this burgeoning industry to chew on as well." *Patti J. Shock, CPCE, Professor and Department Chair, Tourism and Convention Administration, Harrah College of Hotel Administration, University of Nevada–Las Vegas*

CULTURAL TOURISM: THE PARTNERSHIP BETWEEN TOURISM AND CULTURAL HERITAGE MANAGEMENT by Bob McKercher and Hilary du Cros. (2002). "The book brings together concepts, perspectives, and practicalities that must be understood by both cultural heritage and tourism managers, and as such is a must-read for both." *Hisashi B. Sugaya, AICP, Former Chair, International Council of Monuments and Sites, International Scientific Committee on Cultural Tourism; Former Executive Director, Pacific Asia Travel Association Foundation, San Francisco, CA*

TOURISM IN THE ANTARCTIC: OPPORTUNITIES, CONSTRAINTS, AND FUTURE PROSPECTS by Thomas G. Bauer. (2001). "Thomas Bauer presents a wealth of detailed information on the challenges and opportunities facing tourism operators in this last great tourism frontier." *David Mercer, PhD, Associate Professor, School of Geography & Environmental Science, Monash University, Melbourne, Australia*

SERVICE QUALITY MANAGEMENT IN HOSPITALITY, TOURISM, AND LEISURE edited by Jay Kandampully, Connie Mok, and Beverley Sparks. (2001). "A must-read.... a treasure.... pulls together the work of scholars across the globe, giving you access to new ideas, international research, and industry examples from around the world." *John Bowen, Professor and Director of Graduate Studies, William F. Harrah College of Hotel Administration, University of Nevada, Las Vegas*

TOURISM IN SOUTHEAST ASIA: A NEW DIRECTION edited by K. S. (Kaye) Chon. (2000). "Presents a wide array of very topical discussions on the specific challenges facing the tourism industry in Southeast Asia. A great resource for both scholars and practitioners." *Dr. Hubert B. Van Hoof, Assistant Dean/Associate Professor, School of Hotel and Restaurant Management, Northern Arizona University*

THE PRACTICE OF GRADUATE RESEARCH IN HOSPITALITY AND TOURISM edited by K. S. Chon. (1999). "An excellent reference source for students pursuing graduate degrees in hospitality and tourism." *Connie Mok, PhD, CHE, Associate Professor, Conrad N. Hilton College of Hotel and Restaurant Management, University of Houston, Texas*

THE INTERNATIONAL HOSPITALITY MANAGEMENT BUSINESS: MANAGEMENT AND OPERATIONS by Larry Yu. (1999). "The abundant real-world examples and cases provided in the text enable readers to understand the most up-to-date developments in international hospitality business." *Zheng Gu, PhD, Associate Professor, College of Hotel Administration, University of Nevada, Las Vegas*

CONSUMER BEHAVIOR IN TRAVEL AND TOURISM by Abraham Pizam and Yoel Mansfeld. (1999). "A must for anyone who wants to take advantage of new global opportunities in this growing industry." *Bonnie J. Knutson, PhD, School of Hospitality Business, Michigan State University*

LEGALIZED CASINO GAMING IN THE UNITED STATES: THE ECONOMIC AND SOCIAL IMPACT edited by Cathy H. C. Hsu. (1999). "Brings a fresh new look at one of the areas in tourism that has not yet received careful and serious consideration in the past." *Muzaffer Uysal, PhD, Professor of Tourism Research, Virginia Polytechnic Institute and State University, Blacksburg*

HOSPITALITY MANAGEMENT EDUCATION edited by Clayton W. Barrows and Robert H. Bosselman. (1999). "Takes the mystery out of how hospitality management education programs function and serves as an excellent resource for individuals interested in pursuing the field." *Joe Perdue, CCM, CHE, Director, Executive Masters Program, College of Hotel Administration, University of Nevada, Las Vegas*

MARKETING YOUR CITY, U.S.A.: A GUIDE TO DEVELOPING A STRATEGIC TOURISM MARKETING PLAN by Ronald A. Nykiel and Elizabeth Jascolt. (1998). "An excellent guide for anyone involved in the planning and marketing of cities and regions. . . . A terrific job of synthesizing an otherwise complex procedure." *James C. Maken, PhD, Associate Professor, Babcock Graduate School of Management, Wake Forest University, Winston-Salem, North Carolina*

Order a copy of this book with this form or online at:
http://www.haworthpress.com/store/product.asp?sku=5140

COMMUNITY DESTINATION MANAGEMENT IN DEVELOPING ECONOMIES

_____in hardbound at $49.95 (ISBN-13: 978-0-7890-2386-5; ISBN-10: 0-7890-2386-5)

_____in softbound at $34.95 (ISBN-13: 978-0-7890-2387-2; ISBN-10: 0-7890-2387-3)

Or order online and use special offer code HEC25 in the shopping cart.

COST OF BOOKS_____

POSTAGE & HANDLING_____
(US: $4.00 for first book & $1.50 for each additional book)
(Outside US: $5.00 for first book & $2.00 for each additional book)

SUBTOTAL_____

IN CANADA: ADD 7% GST_____

STATE TAX_____
(NJ, NY, OH, MN, CA, IL, IN, PA, & SD residents, add appropriate local sales tax)

FINAL TOTAL_____
(If paying in Canadian funds, convert using the current exchange rate, UNESCO coupons welcome)

☐ **BILL ME LATER:** (Bill-me option is good on US/Canada/Mexico orders only; not good to jobbers, wholesalers, or subscription agencies.)

☐ Check here if billing address is different from shipping address and attach purchase order and billing address information.

Signature_____

☐ **PAYMENT ENCLOSED: $**_____

☐ **PLEASE CHARGE TO MY CREDIT CARD.**

☐ Visa ☐ MasterCard ☐ AmEx ☐ Discover
☐ Diner's Club ☐ Eurocard ☐ JCB

Account # _____

Exp. Date_____

Signature_____

Prices in US dollars and subject to change without notice.

NAME_____

INSTITUTION_____

ADDRESS_____

CITY_____

STATE/ZIP_____

COUNTRY_____ COUNTY (NY residents only)_____

TEL_____ FAX_____

E-MAIL_____

May we use your e-mail address for confirmations and other types of information? ☐ Yes ☐ No
We appreciate receiving your e-mail address and fax number. Haworth would like to e-mail or fax special discount offers to you, as a preferred customer. **We will never share, rent, or exchange your e-mail address or fax number.** We regard such actions as an invasion of your privacy.

Order From Your Local Bookstore or Directly From
The Haworth Press, Inc.
10 Alice Street, Binghamton, New York 13904-1580 • USA
TELEPHONE: 1-800-HAWORTH (1-800-429-6784) / Outside US/Canada: (607) 722-5857
FAX: 1-800-895-0582 / Outside US/Canada: (607) 771-0012
E-mail to: orders@haworthpress.com

For orders outside US and Canada, you may wish to order through your local sales representative, distributor, or bookseller.
For information, see http://haworthpress.com/distributors

(Discounts are available for individual orders in US and Canada only, not booksellers/distributors.)

PLEASE PHOTOCOPY THIS FORM FOR YOUR PERSONAL USE.
http://www.HaworthPress.com   BOF06